Dancing With Creation

Martha Ann Kirk, CCVI

©Copyright 1983 by Resource Publications Inc.
P.O. Box 444
Saratoga, CA 95071.
All Rights Reserved.
Library of Congress 83-6145
ISBN 0-89390-042-7

7/92

Cover Design and Layout: Karen Dewey
Typography: Sandra Ramirez Guerrero
Mechanical Artist: Karen Dewey

Illustrations

Los Danzantes of San Antonio, Texas, under the direction of Mary Guerrero, dancing before the Christmas créche at St. Jude's Church. Photography: Sister Maria Teresa Flores, CCVI. Pages 17, 18, 19, 20, 42, 49.

Misa Criolla presented in St. Elizabeth's church, Oakland, California, by the Dancers' Circle of the Bay Area under the direction of Genia Simpson (4110 El Nido Road, Lafáyette, California 94549). Photography: Jeanette Rodriquez. Pages 24, 50, 53.

Native Americans dancing in front of Mission Dolores in California. Lithograph made by Louis Choris in 1816. Courtesy of Bancroft Library, University of California, Berkeley. Pages 30, 31.

Native Americans of New Mexico dancing for a religious feast. Courtesy of the Maxwell Museum of Anthropology, University of New Mexico, Albuquerque. Pages 34, 35.

Religious Procession, Feast of San Estevan, 1889, Acoma Pueblo. (#1926). Photography: Charles F. Lummis. Courtesy of the Museum of New Mexico, Santa Fe. Page 59.

Los Pastores Players and Matachines dancers at San Jose Mission, San Antonio, Texas. Courtesy of *Today's Catholic.* Pages 62, 63, 66 67.

Conchero Dancer of Andrés Seguda, Our Lady of Guadalupe Church, Laredo, Texas. Courtesy of José Flores Peregrino and Revista Rio Bravo. Page 70.

> Photography: Adrian Collazo. Page 70.

> Angelina Mendez, Conchera Dancer. Photography: Cuate Santos. Page 71.

> Jose Flores Peregrino and Sarah Peregrino. Photography: Adrian Collazo. Page 72.

André Segura, Conchero dancer and leader. Photography: Cuate Santos. Page 74.

Children of St. Elizabeth's Church, Oakland, California. Photography: Martha Ann Kirk, CCVI. Pages 77, 78, 79.

Alleluia danced at the installation of Bishop Ricardo Ramirez, San Antonio, Texas. Photography: Sister Maria Teresa Flores, CCVI. Pages 83, 84, 85, 86.

Los Viejitos. Photography: Phil Smeenge. Page's 87, 90.

Portrait of Martha Ann Kirk. Photography: Phill Smeenge.

To my father Bert
my mother Ada
and my brother Rob

Whose love reveals to me God as father, mother, and brother dancing together and teaching me to dance.

Preface

The prophet Zephaniah spoke of God dancing for joy as on a festival day, rejoicing over the people, and renewing them with love. We are invited to be like God. We are invited to dance and this brings joy, renewal, and love.

In Christian education and worship, today more than ever, there is a need to invite people to involve not just their mind but their whole self. The Bishop's Committee on the Liturgy states:

> Liturgy is total, and therefore must be much
> more than a merely rational or intellectual
> exercise. Valid tradition reflects this attention
> to the whole person. In view of our
> culture's emphasis on reason it is critically
> important for the Church to re-emphasize
> a more total approach to the human person
> by opening up and developing the non-rational
> elements of liturgical celebration:
> the concerns for feelings of conversion,
> support, joy, repentance, trust,
> love, memory, movement, gesture, wonder.[1]

This text suggests prayer in movement and gesture for the whole Christian community and for specialized dancers with whom the community can identify. This is a book not only of dance history and technique, but a book of spirituality: considering how dance is a spiritual discipline, how dance themes reflect biblical themes, and what aspects of Mexican and Native American spiritualities can enrich the whole Christian community today.

Since dance in religious education and worship may seem novel to some persons, this text gives some of the historical tradition of movement in worship and of these particular dances. Scriptural references associated with the dances are given, as well as suggestions for homilies, discussions, or meditations.

Religious dance should be done from the inside out. What a dancer knows deep in his or her heart comes out of feet and fingers. In this text the dances are not explained in elaborate detail for the professional choreographer, but rather the general form and spirit of the dances are described for interested dancers in ordinary congregations. Dancers are invited to enflesh the basic bones of the dances. It is recommended that dance preparation start with meditation on the scriptural text. Then each of the dancers tries improvising movements that convey the main theme of the text. After this, they begin to listen to the music and work out the dance technique from the suggestions given here.

The process of developing the dances, as much as the finished work, can be an experience of prayer. Creative processes make us sensitive to our Creator.

Martha Ann Kirk, CCVI

Feast of St. Teresa of Avila, 1982
Graduate Theological Union
Berkeley, California

Table of Contents

Acknowledgements

I want to express my gratitude to the dancers who have stimulated me to try to articulate a little about their vitality and beauty on these pages.

Many people have sparked my creativity, stretched my mind and body, refined my rambling style, and healed my wounds, especially Doug Adams, Carolyn Deitering, Carla De Sola, James L. Empereur, S.J., Sister Maria Teresa Flores, C.C.V.I., Mary-Sharon Moore, Michael Moynahan, S.J., Catherine Stewart-Roache, and my precious community, the Sisters of Charity of the Incarnate Word. I pray that they may delight in God's surprises and feel God's tender love, both of which they reflect to me.

Introduction

Western religion and culture has been characterized as masculine. The mythical Apollo has been identified as the paradigmatic figure of the West because he symbolizes objectivity, rationality, individuality, clarity, and heightened awareness. Because Western societies have judged this masculine image to be superior to the other side of humanity, the feminine, these characteristics have dominated art and theology. But today there is a movement away from this androcentric vision of the universe with its accompanying devaluation of the feminine with its qualities of gentleness, tenderness, and openness. A process of transformation is taking place which puts premium value on the historical concreteness of our lives, our participation in actual living, and our being embodied personalities. This change, which is grounded in a revitalized recognition of the imagination, constitutes a new religious perspective. It is through the human imagination that we are breaking out of our tyrannical, androcentric way of seeing in order to emerge into a new way of living sexually where masculinity is wedded equally with a revalued feminity. We shall achieve a more human and Wholistic way of living when the composure, coolness, and serene reserve of Apollo is qualified by feminine receptivity, emotional involvement and aesthetic passion.

Martha Ann Kirk's book on dance, especially dance in the Mexican and Native American cultures, provides a way of looking at what is not exclusively Apollonian where the male is the precondition for the understanding of the female. Dance, because it is a form of imaginative embodiment, is one of the most effective ways of overcoming the split between masculine and feminine in our culture and Church. There is nothing wrong with masculine values. Quite the contrary. But problems arise when they are given exclusive priority by societies to the detriment of such feminine principles of form-giving, intuition and relationality. And these difficulties are exacerbated when cultures attempt to make a too clear cut distinction between men and women by assigning masculine traits to the males and feminine traits to the females. The result of this separation is not enlightenment but confusion. Dance in festivities, ritual, and education can help us root out this dichotomous view of the world. A life characterized by either/or, self/other, history/nature, male/female and similar polarities can only be less human. Such inhumanity results from the facile categorization which allots men and women to pre-

determined statuses based on faulty and oversimplified characteriza-
tion. In such a world people are like fixed objects which can be easily
manipulated. It is a static world in which everything has its place in
relation to one unchanging center. This center is the reasonable Apollo (the male) who is the measure of all things. It is a world where men
and women are cut off from their own life stories, their relationships
with others, and their own earthly bodies. What chance has the imagination to inform our lives when surrounded by demands for objectivity and predictability? The imagination is concrete, lives in history,
and overcomes separation within the person through embodiment. It
is predominantly feminine. But this feminine imagination is not the
monopoly of women; with its instinctual drive for community, it must
belong to men as well. In order to rediscover the imagination, we
must move into a limit or boundary situation where the values are not
judged according to norms of superiority, inferiority, or opposition.
We must look for many and moveable centers of living, not one. One
way to explore these new modes of living is dance. Through dance
we revision our lives, we gather our experiences together in meaningful ways, and we break the masculine image which has been im-
perializing us through its aggressive drive toward individuation. Of
course, it is true that one can present dance in an androcentric way,
with a strong emphasis on abstract ideas and cause/effect relationships. But the dance form itself encourages us to move away from
such self-conscious differentiation, from a phallic self-assertion
directed toward accomplishment through conflict. Rather, dance by
means of the imagination helps us to achieve an androgynous self-
understanding, especially as this is filtered through our own his-
toricity, our participation in life processes, and our incarnate natures.

One of the transformations that takes place through dance is the
movement from regarding our personal stories as a series of objective
facts to understanding ourselves as unfolding processes ever in need
of reinterpretation. The past, present, and future are not closed en-
tities. When a person advances in growth, the horizon of the past is in
motion, the horizon of the present is being formed, and the horizon of
the future is experienced in anticipation. In dance, whether we are
performing or not, these horizons are brought together in a tension
where a unified, but still dynamic, life is possible. Newness, related-
ness, and a transformed past are the ingredients of our ongoing stories
when they are enacted in a more feminine style. It is the living of our

12

imaginations that discovers the meaning in the past and present and projects that meaning into the future. Interpretation is as much a part of life as what is being interpreted. Such interpretation takes place whenever we allow reality and the imagination to intertwine in such a way as to transform the past, the present, and the future. For instance, it may be that when we are more accepting of our feminine attributes, we shall more readily identify the areas of injustice in our world. There are forms of oppression which remain hidden to disciplined discrimination and which only feminine wisdom can uncover.

Shared life occurs through dance. It removes the barriers of defensiveness and role-status which we set between ourselves and others. Through dance we allow others to participate in our lives. This is risky because then we define ourselves, to a large degree, in terms of others such as friends and relatives, mentors and lovers, spouses, people with real names and feelings. They are other and they threaten us because we both crave for and fear intimacy at the same time. But shared life when it is imaged as a form of conversation can alleviate much of this fear. Dance assists us to envision life as an event of dialogue where the subject matter takes over and we are lost in the happening. To live humanly is to be in conversation with other. The dialogue of dance takes place in community and dance arises out of community because all true conversation is collaborative. Martha Ann Kirk competently illustrates this in her choice of native dances.

Despite the physical beauty of the masculine Apollo, the androcentric view takes little note of the flesh. The return to the feminine through the imagination is a movement toward embodiment. Even the most abstract dance form is always bounded by concrete particular bodies. Dance is always enfleshed. Moreover, the evocative nature of dance does not permit it to remain at the level of individual self-expression which is more a masculine proclivity. There is in the art of dance and its performance a universal world of meaning which can be shared with others. Whether we dance or watch, we experience our own embodiment through the dancers as they do through us. Our world cannot end with our skins, and our bodies place us in the rhythm of nature, and we emerge with the universe around us. Dance is our paradigm for understanding what it means to be a human being: to have a communal and carnal existence.

13

In the last analysis this book of dances is a religious one. Dance puts us in touch with our stories, our shared life, and our ties to the earth. It is a new way of seeing by means of the imagination. What is seen through this more androgynous vision is the sacred. It is my hope that this book will be one more step in the attempt to relativize the still prevalent model of the masculine worldview. It is not that the masculine is to be replaced, ignored, or subordinated to the feminine. That would be tantamount to expelling the devil, only to have that devil replaced by a legion more. The point is to touch reality, and so the holy, by encountering ourselves and others more imaginatively. This is not a matter of males and females being more open to each other. Rather, our masculinity must meet our femininity wherever it is to be found and our femininity must confront our masculinity whenever in its presence. We shall transform the Apollo in us when we allow the feminine to emerge in ourselves and in others. Perhaps we need to dance more. Shall we take our cue from Martha Ann Kirk?

James L. Empereur, SJ
Berkeley, CA
April, 1983

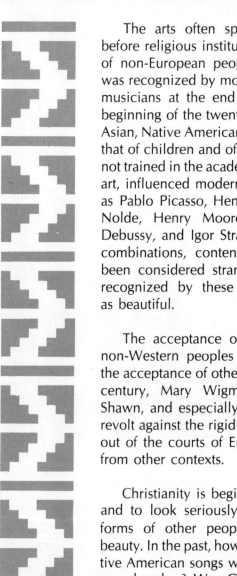

The arts often speak God's prophetic word before religious institutions. The value and beauty of non-European people manifested in their arts was recognized by modern painters, sculptors, and musicians at the end of the late nineteenth and beginning of the twentieth centuries. Folk, African, Asian, Native American, and Oceanic art, as well as that of children and of "primitives," that is, persons not trained in the academic conventions of Western art, influenced modern artists and musicians such as Pablo Picasso, Henri Matisse, Paul Klee, Emile Nolde, Henry Moore, Käthe Kollwitz, Claude Debussy, and Igor Stravinsky. Forms, styles, color combinations, content, and harmonies that had been considered strange, naive, and crude were recognized by these prophetic insightful artists as beautiful.

The acceptance of folk dance and dance of non-Western peoples somewhat parallels that of the acceptance of other arts. In the early part of this century, Mary Wigman, Isadora Duncan, Ted Shawn, and especially Martha Graham began the revolt against the rigidity of classical ballet coming out of the courts of Europe, by using movements from other contexts.

Christianity is beginning to follow these artists and to look seriously at the musical and dance forms of other people and to recognize their beauty. In the past, how many Asian, African, or Native American songs were found in the hymnals of our churches? Was German, French, Italian, and English music intrinsically holy while the music of these other peoples was not? If any instruments could have a claim to being holy from the longest tradition of use in religious services, they would be the drum, the flute, and the tambourine. The organ

was a later secular instrument that was only slowly and with controversy allowed in Christian worship. The language of the Church is that of Pentecost: the languages of all the diverse peoples express the Word of God.

If we wish to challenge our Christian communities to accept peoples of other cultures as brothers and sisters in the family of God, why not use Latin American, Asian, African, or Native American dance in our worship interchangeably with dance from the European ballet or the American modern dance tradition? Using visual art, music, and dance of diverse cultures in worship may need some explanation, but this can be an opportunity for explaining the universality of God's love and revelation. At times when immigrants from Latin countries and Asian countries raise questions in society, it can be noted that most North Americans today are immigrants who have invaded the land of the Native Americans. Basically all people need to remember the words of Leviticus: "If a stranger lives with you in your land, do not molest him. You must count him as one of your own country men and love him as yourself — for you were once strangers yourselves in Egypt. I am Yahweh your God" (Leviticus 19:33-34).

Scripture also speaks of dance to celebrate the movement from one situation to another. The dance of Miriam celebrated the move-

ment from the slavery of Egypt towards the promise of a land flowing with milk and honey (see Exodus 15:20-21). In this passage, considered by many scholars one of the oldest parts of scripture, a woman led the community in prayer through her dance. Dancing is a way of appropriating and affirming freedom and thanking God for it. People who have been oppressed in one way or another reclaim their dignity and liberty as children of God in the energy of dance. Jeremiah spoke of the joy that the Hebrews would feel when they would be allowed to leave the captivity of Babylon and return to their native Israel: "Adorned once more, and with your tambourines, you will go out dancing gaily" (Jeremiah 31:4).

Saint Augustine said: "One who sings, prays twice." It could be added: "One who dances, prays thrice," because the intensity of involvement to which Augustine alludes is even greater when persons use their whole body, and not just their voice. As the rhythm of the distant moon stimulates the rhythm of the tides, so persons can be attracted and animated by rhythm. The rhythms of handclapping, of drums, of marachas, or of other percussive instruments are ways of building unity in a congregation. Often these are used merely as a background for singing, but they are good alone to lead a group into a

reflective mood, perhaps in tune with their heartbeats or to excite a group to a festive mood. Simple swaying, processional steps, or arms gesturing to a Native American drum beat or a lively Latin beat can be used very effectively.

Motion is contagious. If someone in a group stretches, yawns, or begins to tap his or her foot, how often others unconsciously imitate. Whirlwinds, waterfalls, and rivers have rhythm and dynamic forms. Only in motion can they be; if they stopped, they would change to a calm or a lake. The psalmist speaks of the dance of creation: the floods clap their hands, the mountains rejoice like goats, and the hills skip like lambs. In the dynamism, in the process, in the fluidity, in the dance they exist; and so it is with our own lives. We have no frozen moments. We cannot stop the clock. We cannot stop the motion. Even in times of apparent rest our heart, brain, and lungs continue their rhythmic dance. So our lives are dances before God. Do we try to learn the movement, the rhythm, and the steps from God? Do we, like Jonah, try to move in the opposite direction; or like Job, curse that our dance of life began and pray that it might end? Do we drag behind God our partner, refusing to let go and be carried freely, open to the momentum and moments of ecstasy? Do we rush before God our partner, missing the subtle joy of rhythm, bumping into obstacles, and tripping as we withdraw from centering? and the Center? Worship can be practice for the dance of life. Human life is the substance of worship.

Mexican And Native American Religious Dance

In the areas of the American continents called New Spain, both Spaniards and Christian natives danced for special occasions such as Easter, Christmas, and for the feasts of Corpus Christi, of Mary, and of patron saints. Story dances, dances of praise, processional dances, and dances which illustrated the triumph of good over evil were used in the new land as in Europe. Though the records of dance in the early middle ages in Spain are sparse, there are links with the dance themes and forms of the first Christian centuries. These ancient themes are alive in Mexico and the southwestern United States today. Often the dances have fused with and been enriched by Native American dances.

The tradition of Christian dance is harder to trace than that of Christian art or music. While some paintings and some hymn verses remain from the first centuries, dance is an ephemeral art which leaves no outlines. Two of the earliest sources describing Christian liturgy, the writings of St. Justin Martyr (c. 150 A.D.) and of St. Hippolytus (c. 200 A.D.) mention the joyful types of dances used in liturgy. Three fourth-century leaders praise the dance that was used in their worship: Basilius, bishop of Caesarea, St Ambrose, bishop of Milan, and St. John Chrysostom, patriarch of Constantinople.

The Council of Toledo, which discouraged rowdy and inappropriate dancing for feast days, encouraged St. Isidore of Seville to compose a ritual with elaborate movement in 678. This ritual, which included boys dancing, was incorporated in the Mozarabic Mass. During the centuries this elaborate liturgy was discontinued in most places, but the dances which are still done on Shrove Tuesday, Corpus Christi, and the Immaculate Conception in the Cathedral of Seville in front of the high altar come from this ancient tradition. When a conservative archbishop wished to stop the dances in 1439, the people supported the dancers going to Rome to seek the approval of Pope Eugenius IV. The pope saw nothing offensive in what they were doing and said that they should be allowed to continue dancing before the altar. Originally, the boys who performed the dancing were dressed as angels, echoing the idea of St. Clement of Alexandria that liturgical dance reflects the dance of the angels around the throne of God. In later centuries the dancers began to wear the dress of pages and to play castanets. Different patterns and songs for the dance have been used through the centuries. At the time America was settled, similar dances before the Blessed Sacrament were done in Toledo, Valencia, and Yepes.

Spain has had more dance associated with Christian worship than any other European country, so it was quite natural that the priests and settlers continued to dance in New Spain when they came in the sixteenth century. After centuries of occupation and many civil wars, a great flowering of dance took place in Spain when the Moors were expelled. The whole country seemed to dance with joy. While religious dance was somewhat suppressed in many countries as the rational element in religion was over-developed at the expense of the intuitive, Spain continued the dance. The Church, eager to educate, encouraged medieval miracle and morality plays with dance at the time when these were beginning to fade out in the rest of Europe. These were done both in the church buildings and nearby. The archives of Toledo Cathedral in 1415 describe the type of dances, costumes, and music for a certain feast day as well as how the dancers were to be rewarded for their services.

One play from this period told the story of the Annunciation in a *pas de deux* done by the Holy Spirit and Mary. During this period of Spanish freedom from the Moors, the Spaniards had just begun to use the *pas de deux,* in which a man lifts a woman into the air. It was interpreted to mean that woman's dignity was elevated and a man no longer had supreme rights over her. Also from this period comes a dance still done today, in which a group representing the rich dances with a group representing the poor, and they then change places. Dance, then and now, has great power to cut across social barriers and unite people. From the fifth through the twelfth century in Christianity there was a progressive tendency to isolate clergy from and put them above the whole Christian community. While in the early Church all had danced together, priests began to dance only with other priests, deacons with deacons. This parallels the practice of liturgy as something holy which was done by clergy alone, and people could only be distant spectators — they could not really participate. Many of the objections to dance in worship then, as today, are based on the correct understanding that dance unites all in a common priesthood and the one Body of Christ.

From the early Middle Ages many Church festivals were celebrated with processions, and these processions usually involved dance. In some, all the people did rhythmic steps together, and in others the processions stopped along the way while more elaborate dances were done. Dance — that is, embodied worship — was particularly appropriate for the feast of Corpus Christi which celebrates the Body of Christ. In Barcelona, Valencia, and Mallorca the Dance of the Eagles continues to be used for that festival and others. The eagle, representing the evangelist John who soars to mystical heights, moves before the procession and then dances before the altar. From the seventeenth century until the beginning of the twentieth century in Madrid, Burgos, and Santiago di Compostela, "giants" and "dwarfs," grotesque figures with masks of papier-mache, danced in the Corpus Christi procession and stood for the forces of evil that were being driven out by the presence of Christ. Some places had allegorical dances that involved devils being suppressed as in mystery plays. In Valencia children did a pantomime dance fighting these evil spirits as the toreadors fight the bulls. Occasionally the children would dance toward the sacrament to be strengthened in their battle with evil. In Onna twelve young dancers would kneel in front of the Blessed Sacrament, then dance ahead, turn, run back, and kneel. Some dance historians believe that the Church deserves credit for the quality of dance in Spain for several centuries, because in continuously sponsoring dance and being critical of rowdy or inappropriate dance, the Church encouraged a high standard of dance performance.

Dance has also been used on the vigils of feast days to prepare people for the coming day. Hymns were written for people to dance during their all-night vigil in the church of St. Mary in Montserrat. The people of Nules would dance by a bonfire in front of the church on Christmas eve, and those of Mallorca would dance through the streets on Midsummer eve to commemorate St. John the Baptist.

Following the ideas of St. Ambrose and other early theologians that dance affirmed Christians' faith in the Resurrection, people of the early Church would dance at the graves of the martyrs. Throughout the centuries these ideas inspired dance in Spain at wakes and after burials. Sometimes persons cried as they danced, but their movement affirmed their faith in the resurrection. In New Spain also dance was used to deal creatively with death, particularly in the observance of All Saints and All Souls Days.

Then, as today, dance is a very healthy emotional release in times of great pain or stress. Though dance can be abused, it is one of the most effective ways of building community and good morale. The Spanish Church seemed to recognize this and, though there were occasional prohibitions of excessive or inappropriate dancing, generally dance was appreciated.

Saint Ignatius of Loyola, the famous Spaniard of the sixteenth century and founder of the Jesuit order which played a significant role in bringing Christianity to America, often gave persons spiritual direction while he was a student at the University of Paris after being wounded and converted. One day a friend who was very depressed asked Ignatius to do some of the dances of the saint's native Basque region to try to help him. Though Ignatius limped, he danced to please the friend and thus drove the depression away. Did Ignatius teach his companion Jesuits and those who followed to give spiritual consolation and support in the same way? Perhaps such embodied expressions of the good news could be used more in spiritual direction today.

Elaborate ballets were created to celebrate the beatification of St. Ignatius of Loyola in 1609 and to celebrate the canonization of St. Charles Borromeo in 1610. Descriptions of these are given by Claude Francois Menestrier, a French Jesuit, in his book *Des Ballets Anciennes et Modernes*, published in Parish in 1682. Since the Jesuits which Ignatius founded were carrying the gospel to Europe, Asia, Africa, and America, persons representing these showed their gratitude in dance. The American troupe included a dance of young children dressed as parrots and monkeys, fowl and animals of New Spain which delighted the Europeans. The Jesuits have always used the arts in evangelization, and they contributed substantially to the history of ballet in their development of religious ballets and dramas during the seventeenth century.

Saint Teresa of Avila, another great Spanish spiritual leader of the sixteenth century and a reformer of the Carmelite order, delighted in spirited dancing and encouraged her sisters to whole-heartedly celebrate the goodness of God. There are records of dances performed before the Blessed Sacrament in the Carmelite convent in Dijon, France, and such dance may have been used in many other convents.

Many civilizations developed on the American continents for thousands of years before the Spanish settlers arrived. These native peoples from Alaska to the tip of South America had a great variety of religious beliefs and practices. They did not distinguish between sacred and profane aspects of life. The natural world and human life were animated by spiritual powers. The people transmitted their religious stories through ritual with music and dance. Dance was prayer. Even contemporary Spanish vocabulary reveals the religious associations of dance. *Bailar* refers to social dancing including that of couples, while another verb, *danzar*, refers to the older meaning of dance as ritual.

Constance Fisher in *Dancing the Old Testament* writes of Hebrew religious dance in three main categories: 1) the rhythm of life and death, that is, of the main stages and passages in life; 2) the rhythm of ecstatic response, as the experiences of the early prophets or of people celebrating triumphs; and 3) the rhythm of nature, the dances of the cycles of the year. Most of the dances of the Native Americans have the same underlying themes. The natives had dances associated with the life cycle, that is dances for birth, puberty, marriage, sickness, and death. Native peoples, aware of both the opportunity and the challenge of the times of transition in life, the liminal times, danced out these moments to sanctify them.

Moreover, Native Americans had many types of ecstatic dances, such as vision dances for enlightenment, dances to build up energy for war or to celebrate victory, or dances for purification. At the time the Spaniards settled in Mexico the Aztecs had elaborate dances on religious festivals in which about a thousand persons participated, moving in concentric circles. The religious and political leaders in elaborate ceremonial garments, as well as the ordinary people, joined in prayer. The more important persons would be in the inner circles. The dances began with slow music in low tones, gradually increasing to faster movements and higher pitched melodies. This description suggests that these dances, rather than being narratives, as many dances were, developed religious fervor leading to ecstasy. Further, the people had particular dances for the seasons to implore that animals might be plentiful or that crops would be abundant. Corn, bean, buffalo, deer, sun, and rain dances were very common. Even today among the Tarahumaras in northern Mexico the same word is used for work and for dance. While some of these people go out to plant the crops, others dance all day, a prayer that the planting may be fruitful. When the hunts or the harvests were successful, the people danced in celebration and gratitude that they had been blessed with the goods necessary for life.

Bernal diaz del Castillo whose journal recorded the sixteenth century conquest of Mexico described the skilled dancers and tumblers who performed for Montezuma, the Aztec ruler. The native codices of the time depicted the various dances; the people had a variety of wind and percussive instruments. Xochipili or Macuil-xochitl was the Aztec god of music, dance, love, and flowers. Among these people who respected education, beauty, and the arts the Spaniards established themselves. The leader of the Spaniards, Hernando Cortez, directed that children of the important native families come to what is now Mexico City for a Christian education.

Latin cultures have tended to recognize the value of the arts in education and in life. The Spaniards brought a great respect for the arts with them to New Spain. The Academy of San Carlos was founded in Mexico City to develop painters and sculptors. A number of religious dramas were presented by a friar, Toribeo de Benevente, in Tlaxcala in 1538. When Juan De Onate, the explorer, reached the banks of the Rio Grande and claimed the adjoining land for Spain on April 30, 1598, there was a Mass, a sermon, and a play to celebrate the occasion. Missionaries and soldiers as well as settlers considered the arts essential. Unfortunately, the Europeans did not often appreciate the art, architecture, dance, drama, and music of the native peoples, and sometimes suppressed or destroyed them. Despite this cultural bias, native peoples under Spanish influence continued to produce more arts than natives under the other European settlers. Rich mestizo, which blended native and Spanish styles, and native styles, have continued.

An early example of blended cultures were the religious dance pageants started by Fray Pedro de Gante. The friar, one of the first Franciscans to go to New Spain, was frustrated in his attempts to get the native peoples to memorize the concepts of Christianity. Finally he recognized that their own religions had been kept alive through the centuries through ritual song and dance, and he decided to adapt

par Jacquelin d'après Choris.

Danse des habitans de Califo...

30

Lith de Langlumé r. de l'Abbaye. N 4

la mission de S Francisco.

their music, dance, and drama to tell Christian stories. The happy friar recounted his success in a letter that he wrote to King Philip II on June 23, 1558. Fray Pedro began with the Christmas story and found that the dance pageants were so appealing that the people were choosing to come to Christianity. Before, they were often coerced.

While pastoral missionaries like Fray Pedro de Gante respected and used the richness of native culture, distant legislators were not always as sensitive. In 1623 an office of the Inquisition suggested that communities which used drums for religious songs should be fined for keeping up pagan traditions. Despite occasional opposition like this, Spanish ideas and forms influenced the arts of the Native Americans and the native ideas and forms influenced the Spanish. The fandango which became a very popular dance in Spain during the late seventeenth century was related to the Reinos de las Indias which the explorers learned from the natives of the continent they first thought was India.

Music, dance, and pageantry were used by the Franciscans who worked among Native Americans in what is today Texas, New Mexico, Arizona, and California. Letters and journals which describe life in the mission of San Jose in San Antonio, Texas, which was founded in 1720 and used until 1824, speak of the Matachines dances done for Christmas and for Corpus Christi. The friars encouraged these dances which were used in Spain for special occasions. The dancers wore masks, long robes, often a headdress of flowers, and carried a rattle or pronged stick. Groups of the dancers were considered defenders of religion. Violin music was used with the rhythmic percussion of the rattles they carried. While this dance was sanctioned by the missionaries, their writings sometimes criticize the natives' mitotes, rituals with dance done in the woods in which the people invoked magic. Processions, a basic form of dance, were done every Saturday and on special feasts as well. Glass lanterns and beautiful statues were carried, and the people walked in two lines playing instruments and singing the rosary sometimes to music they had composed. One observer noted that their music was so sweet and their pleasure in doing this so great that other non-believing natives were attracted to become Christians as well. When all the harvest had been gathered, the people decorated the last cart of food. Then they went through the mission complex in joyful procession, singing in thanksgiving to God.

Padre Junipero Serra, who received permission from Spain to found missions in California in 1769, was a good singer and felt that a love of music was an important link with the native peoples. Until the California missions were secularized in 1834, the Franciscans who followed Serra taught the peoples to build instruments, as well as sing and play. Some of the padres wrote hymns and masses in styles that would be more suited to the Native American styles than the complex compositions from Spain and South America. Alabados, popular hymns of praise to God welcoming a new day, were commonly sung as they had been in the streets of Spain through the centuries. Padre Florencio Ibanez composed music for Los Pastores, a musical play that was traditionally used in many of the missions on Christmas eve. The custom of dramatizing the shepherds' journey to see the Christ child comes from the medieval miracle and morality plays used in churches to teach people. While it is hard to determine if or which dances were done inside the mission churches of California, a lithograph done by Louis Choris in 1816 depicts native dances in front of Mission Dolores. The native people of the community and the Europeans are gathered, enjoying the dances. Dramatic touches were used in the liturgy at different times of the year, such as at Pentecost. The wooden music stand, which can still be seen at Mission San Juan Bautista, has a box in which white doves were hidden. They were released during Mass to symbolize the coming of the Holy Spirit. In some churches during the Middle Ages both rose petals and doves were released from the choir.

New Mexico and Arizona, which have had continuous communities of Native American peoples, have also had continuous traditions of Native American dance. New Mexico in fact has descendants of the Spaniards who have continued the processions, plays, music, and dance in Santa Fe, Albuquerque, and other towns. In the pueblo of Isleta on Christmas eve a dance is done around the Christ child in the manger. The dancers breathe over the image of the Christ child, symbolically absorbing his Spirit. The Hebrew word for spirit in scripture, ruhah, also means air, wind, breath.

In some pueblos like San Felipe the Buffalo dance is done in the

church after Midnight Mass. Almost all pueblos have dances on Christmas eve and Christmas day. Saint Francis of Assisi legendarily began the use of the Christmas crèche to bring the story of the gospel to life for simple persons. Also, he is said to have started the practice of dancing carols around the crib. This association with St. Francis may be one of the reasons why dancing at Christmas was so popular in Christian communities formed by the Franciscans.

In Taos pueblo the Deer dance has been done on the feast of the Epiphany. . The Corn dance, which is a prayer for a good harvest, that for life, is begun in some pueblos on Easter. Sometimes a statue of Christ or a saint to whom the people have special devotion is carried out in procession to the place where the dances are done. The statue is typically placed in a shrine called a ramada, made of cedar and juniper branches. Many of the pueblos, such as Isleta, Cochiti, Jemez, Laguna, Picuris, Sandia, San Felipe, San Ildefonso, San Juan, Santa Ana, Santa Clara, Santo Domingo, and Taos, celebrate the feast of their patron saints with dances all day.

Ritual dances of Mexico and the southwestern United States are in continuity with both Spanish and Native American traditions of re-ligious dance and provide a living link with the worship of the early Christian centuries. Early Christians used dance to celebrate that life triumphs over death in Christ's resurrection, that good triumphs over the forces of evil, and that creation reflects God and is the instrument through which God blesses people. They danced on the feast days commemorating Christ's birth and life and the days commemorating his friends. All parts of the Christian heritage including its rich tradi-tion of dance can contribute to Christian spirituality today.

Native American Spirituality and Ecology

Native American spiritualities with their dances can lead to more holistic worship in the sense of concern for the whole earth and concern for the whole person, body and spirit. While the Judeo-Christian scriptures have described the water, the land, the plants, the animals, fish,· and fowl as created by God and called "good" by God, there has been a lack of emphasis on persons as stewards in harmony with a creation belonging to God. While the original Hebrew text of God's command to humankind is a call to responsibility and care, it is often translated: "Fill the earth and subdue it" (Genesis 1:28). This translation has been used to justify the heirarchical approach that persons are above animal life which is above vegetative life which is above inanimate matter. Often there is less and less consideration of the intrinsic respect owed each category as one goes "down" the chain. Western Christianity has often taught an almost exclusive transcendentalism, a dualism of body and soul, and a preoccupation with fallen nature. It has used the imagery of a spiritual father God of the heavens who dominates over the material mother earth. Native American spiritualities have respected the presence of divine power in the earth as well as in the heavens. Christianity, influenced by Greek Orphism and Neoplatonism, which separate soul and body, has often forgotten its Jewish roots, which affirm the whole person. We have deceived ourselves in thinking that our minds and spirits are separated from and above material creation, and thus we could rape the earth but still remain pure. Our ecological and sociological problems cannot be solved by technology alone: they call for a renewed spirituality, one in which persons know themselves as interdependent with nature.

Not only is the Creator not indifferent to the quality and respect for life in this world, but "not one sparrow falls to the earth" without the Creator's knowledge and concern. God is not an outside force which punishes persons who abuse each other or the world but persons who fail to respect creation bring destruction upon themselves. The vivid description of Isaiah could be applied to current ecological problems:

> The earth mourns and fades,
> the world languishes and fades;
> both heaven and earth languish.
> The earth is polluted because of its inhabitants,
> who have transgressed laws,
> violated statutes,
> broken the ancient covenant.
> Therefore a curse devours the earth,
> and its inhabitants pay for their guilt;
>
> therefore they who dwell on earth turn pale,
> and few men are left.
> The wine mourns, the vine languishes;
> all the merry-hearted groan.
> Stilled are the cheerful timbrels,
> ended the shouts of the jubilant,
> stilled is the cheerful harp (Isaiah 24:4-8).

The music of the dancers is silent because creation no longer smiles forth plenty, but rather cries out in pain.

An elderly Native American woman who saw where the surface of the earth had been devastated by irresponsible strip miners said that everywhere the white person had touched the earth, the earth was sore. Ravaging the land without regard to its spirit was sacrilegious to the Native American. Killing an animal, catching a fish, or cutting a tree were not to be done without reason. Respect for each, with its indwelling spirit, was important. In *I Heard the Owl Call My Name* by Margaret Craven, the native woman explained to the cedar tree that she only wanted a little of its bark for a baby's blanket and a mat, and that she would not leave it naked. Another Native American woman shared memories of asking her grandmother for a drink of water before going to bed. The grandmother would ask the spirit of the water to allow her to use it. This can be looked upon as superstition and empty ritual, but the approach stands in sharp contrast to contemporary society which often pollutes lakes, rivers, and streams without reflection and thus without responsibility. Water is an image of God's bounteous goodness: "I will open up rivers on the bare heights, and fountains in the broad valleys: I will turn the desert into a marshland and the dry ground into springs of water" (Isaiah 41:18).

Christian rituals using water can take on new meaning when explained in the light of Native American dances for rain or rituals like the one of the grandmother speaking to the good spirit who was recognized in the moment of taking water. Making the sign of the cross on one's self with holy water when entering a church or sprinkling people with water can be dances praising God for life-giving water. Dance comes from a people in rhythm and harmony with the earth around them. Or it comes from a people who seek the harmony of the creation — who wish for rain, for health, for food. We need the dances of Native Americans in our churches today because we are fast losing the rhythm and harmony of natural creation in our concrete and synthetic environments. We must try to learn parts of the old dances and from their vitality make new ones in continuity with their spirit. Dances are considered ways of uniting and healing creatures and creation. They bring wholeness. A Mohawk spiritual leader invited groups at a university where he was visiting to join him in the Fish dance as a way of healing the pollution affecting fish today. Each local church can identify which parts of its environment are most in need of healing. Prayer animated by dance could focus on the needy parts. Movement prayer often helps people to move into effective action.

A group of Native Americans in New Mexico were greatly offended when the area in front of the church where they danced was paved over and their feet could not touch the good earth. Some native peoples cut a hole in the sole of each new moccasin that they may have contact with the good earth. As water, wine, bread, and oil in our sacraments give us a tactile sense of the presence of divine life, so the earth also is a basic symbol of the bounteous goodness of God. If we minimize our contact with that symbol it is difficult to be nurtured by it. If possible, invite your congregation to take off shoes and socks and to stand, to walk, then to dance on the earth or the grass. What is the temperature, the texture, the humidity, and the durability of it? What memories does it evoke? What present meaning does touching the earth have? To what future visions and dances does this lead? What is comfortable, and what is uncomfortable in this contact? What resists, what yields to the shape of the soles of our feet? When and how is it better to be supported, and when and how is it better to be yielded to? Firm earth supports buildings, soft earth allows seed to grow. In which does one delight?

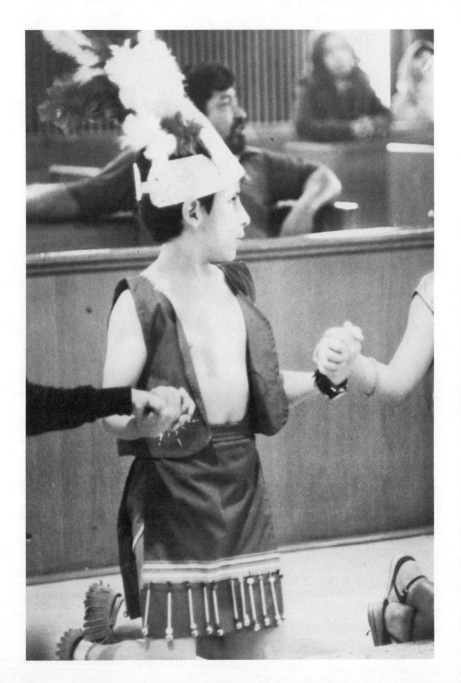

Dancing To Laugh

Joy And Humor In Ritual

God delights in us and invites us to delight in life. Basic movements which persons already do in church, but often unthinkingly or half-heartedly, can take on rich meanings when explained as part of a joyous dance of life. In Mexican culture the greeting for friends and family is not a mere smile or handshake, but a warm embrace, an abrazo. This expansive gesture conveys and reflects a culture that has traditionally valued persons more than things, a culture that has placed great value on family relationships, and a culture that is not afraid of touch. Contemporary psychologists have written about the human need to be touched, which is almost like a need for food or rest. The gesture of peace in worship can be understood as a dance of abrazos, a whole-hearted hug, not afraid of touching the other's body, but rather celebrating all the parts of the Body of Christ.

The holy is never very far from the hilarious. Job struggled with a God who was more of a trickster than a sensible person, and Paul was astonished about a God who would give away all, "taking the form of a slave." God is uncontrollable and unpredictable. As high as the heavens are above the earth are God's ways above ours. The personification of God, Wisdom, delighted in "playing among the children." Some of the greatest religious wisdom of the world is an invitation to playfulness. An ancient proverb says that there is no laughter in hell. Perhaps heaven is where there is laughter. Good rituals that evoke laughter show that the reign of God is in our midst. When the threat of a nuclear holocaust, the bleakness of poverty, and the forces of oppression surround us, laughter is one of the strongest affirmations of faith and hope.

In the polished proper dancer we can see grace and beauty beyond our ability and this gives us insight into the transcendent. But we also need to see the clown dancer in whose foibles and clumsiness we recognize our weakness and our humanness. These are also where we meet God. The clowns poke fun at power, wealth, sex, even religious practice — all the things we can make into idols. Saint Teresa of Avila has said that the best way to deal with the devil is to laugh at him because he hates that; laughter does have a way of disarming forces of evil.

In both Native American dance in the southwestern United States and in folk and ritual dance of Mexico, clowns and humorous figures play an important role. Clowns tease, surprise, disrupt, and seem to subtrovert the ceremonies. Yet in reality their popularity and importance are as great as, if not greater than, that of shamans or priests. In the Feast of Fools in medieval Europe, dignitaries of Church and state were satirized, and the prestigious of this earth could be relativized in relation to ultimate meaning. Seeds of this remained in Spanish customs When the Spaniards came to America their records of Montezuma's court reveal that the Aztecs had court jesters who danced and entertained. They also had humorous characters in religious ceremonies. Humorous mimes and dancers from the Spanish and the native tradition stimulated each other.

Many of the dances mentioned in this text, such as the Spanish giants, dwarfs, and animals in processions, the Los Pastores character, the Viejitos, and the Matachine and Conchero devil antics, are humorous. In the Native American Kachina ceremonies in the pueblos of the southwest the clowns called koshares are very important characters. The koshares are responsible for teaching the dance and seeing that it is done correctly. They often instruct the very young dancers during the ceremony and this does not interrupt since clowns have a freedom that performers do not have.

One of the strongest uses of humor in the Mexican tradition is in the observance of el dia de los muertos, the day of the dead, which actually includes both All Saints Day and All Souls Day, November 1 and 2. When the Spaniards arrived, the natives honored a God of death who was depicted with carved skulls. While death always holds fears, the people basically looked upon it as a natural part of the life cycle process and a transition opening to transformed life. They believed that the spirits of the dead returned to visit with their families at a time of the year that coincided with the Christian rememberance of the dead on All Saints and All Souls Days. This was and continues to be a time for families to be together, gratefully remembering the deceased, and sharing special foods, parties, and dances. It is traditional to buy a candy skull with one's name on it and often cards are sent with calaveras, funny pictures of skeletons. Folk ceramics and children's toys of skeletons doing everyday work, singing, dancing, or playing music, are very common. None of this is morbid; in fact, it is quite humorous. Mexican children grow up with a healthy familiarity with death that children of other cultures often do not have.

In medieval Europe the Church sometimes used the Dance of Death as a teaching device. Death personified would take partner after partner to be with him, irrespective if they were bar maiden or queen, wealthy or poor. Though Mexican folk art sometimes illustrates this type of dance, the most common dances for festival are the Matachine and Conchero dances. Dancing skeletons, sweet tasting skulls, family picnics in the cemetery, and children's toys seem to affirm Paul's words: "O death, where is your victory? O death, where is your sting?" (I Corinthians 15:55). Mexican faith is resurrection faith. In the midst of suffering, poverty, and the forces of death, fiestas are celebrated. The forces of evil cannot prevail for those who love God. Despite the problems and hardships of life, there is an understanding of the nearness of God as in the words of Zephaniah:

Zion, have no fear,
do not let your hands fall limp.
Yahweh your God is in your midst,
a victorious warrior.
He will exult with joy over you,
he will renew you by his love;
he will dance with shouts of joy for you
as on a day of festival (Zephaniah 3:16-18).

God dances for us and invites us to dance in a fiesta.

Other types of humorous dances that are done frequently in Mexico are the combat dances, "the Moors and the Christians," and "St. James." These involve mock battles and very funny looking horses attached to the dancers' bodies. When the sixteenth-century natives first saw the Spaniards on horseback they thought that horse and rider were one creature, and this is the origin of the costumes with attached horses. The dances are interspersed with texts that mingle stories of the Spanish victory over the natives in Mexico with stories of the Spanish victory over the Moors in Spain. Spain has many stories of St. James the apostle who legendarily evangelized the country, returning in later centuries to help the people drive out the Moors. He is called Santiago Matamoros, killer of the Moors. Mexican legends recount fourteen different times when Santiago appeared in Mexico. Through his miraculous intervention the natives submitted to the Christian Spaniards. While these dances are certainly of historical interest and express the apocalyptic dramatic victory motif that is important in Hispanic art and literature, it is questionable whether Christian churches today should encourage arts based on themes of war and re-religious intolerance.

Throughout the ages dance and drama have been used by religious peoples to recount their stories. In planning Christian worship today the first question is: "What is our story, and how are different aspects of it brought out through the year?" Second: "What are our most important celebrations?" And third: "How can dance and drama emphasize and clarify what should be emphasized?"

The Easter season is our most important celebration. The resurrection of Christ is an affirmation of life. The whole liturgical cycle of Lent, Easter, Ascension, and Pentecost focuses on different aspects of the mystery of Easter. We remember Christ's life and we see it continued in the Church as old members are renewed and new ones are born in the waters of baptism. Christ's life is released in the Spirit, as a blessing to all the nations. Western medieval and renaissance painting often graphically depicted Pentecost with hideous-looking creatures fleeing through the air as the wind and fire of God's Spirit released the ultimate and definitely triumphant power for good to overcome evil in the world. This complex of mysteries and symbols pertaining to birth, life, the fertility of the earth, death transformed, and the triumph of good over evil opens many possibilities for dance during the Easter season. Next to the Lord's day, Easter was the first feast in Christianity and was celebrated during the first century after Christ. Only in later centuries, to compete with the Roman pagan festival of light, did Christmas come to be celebrated. We should use the most and the best dances for the Easter season.

While other feasts popular in a certain geographic area should be respected, the Resurrection as the center of biblical Christianity and the Easter season as the primary time of the liturgical year should receive the greatest emphasis in the arts.

Persons may have to be challenged to recognize this since religion in the past may have allowed the peripheral to be central. This task may not be as difficult as it seems, because it is not one of denying the holy in local customs, folklore, dance, and art. It is rather deeply respecting these and searching them for some of their deepest symbolic meaning. When this is done, popular devotion often reveals the central mysteries in Christian description of God and divine involvement with the world. Much dance is based on themes of life, love and nature. All peoples seek life in its fullness, they seek happiness; love gives meaning, and human relationships are an opening to divine relationships. Jesus said: "I have come so that they may have life and have it to the full" (John 10:10). All forms of life can be celebrated. The earth and the animals are part of God's bounty. The cycles of the

year can be a constant reminder of God's ever-renewing life and love.

As in the cycle of the Church's year dance and drama may be used to emphasize those parts which are special; in an individual service the arts are appropriate to emphasize what is more important. While a pastoral sensitivity should be shown to persons who may have misconceptions about the focus of worship, good leadership in liturgy and in liturgical arts should try not to use dance or drama built on the less important parts of a worship service because it distorts what is happening. Processionals and recessionals are usually appropriate because gathering to worship and then being sent forth to share the good news are natural movements in the service. A high point of all Christian worship is the proclamation of the Word of God, and ideally the architecture of a church, the art work used for that occasion, and the music, dance, or drama, should all point to and help clarify the scriptural message. The passage can be developed in dance or dramatic scenarios. The sermon can be presented in dance, that is, "embodied words." At other times it may not be appropriate to dance the words of scripture, but dance preceding the reading of scripture drawing the community's attention to the book of the Word can be very helpful.

Dance can be a reflective pause which opens in the ears of our hearts. This has always been recognized in the Coptic rite, and ancient Christian form of prayer and ceremony which may even antedate the Roman rite. Dance is often used with the gospel to clarify how joyous our response to the good news should be. When Coptic bishops at the Second Vatican Council took their turns leading the services and had dance to celebrate the gospel, many Christians were surprised by this type of prayer. Such an embodied display of joy was certainly as valid and as beautiful, if not more so, than the movements in the rites of European origin.

As the proclamation of the Word of God is of major importance in Christian worship, so also is the eucharistic prayer. In this we remember God's goodness through the ages, we praise God, give thanks, and celebrate Christ's presence among us symbolized by bread and wine. Scripture speaks of the eternal Word of God made visible through Christ's flesh:

> Something which has existed since the beginning,
> that we have heard,
> and we have seen with our own eyes;
> that we have watched
> and touched with our hands:
> the Word, who is life —
> this is our subject.
> That life was made visible (I John 1:1-2).

For the Johannine author the flesh of Christ gave grounding to faith and kept people from being led astray by spiritual cults which were not truly Christan because they denied the Incarnation. In Christian worship today the experience of moving our own flesh in congregational dance and identifying with the movements of the dance-prayer leaders helps us to live this Johannine incarnational theology and not practice heresies which affirm only the soul and not the body.

If there are any parts of Christian worship in which dance, "body prayer," would seem to be most appropriate, they are the eucharistic prayer and communion because in these we remember God's intervention in material creation and the ultimate glorification of creation in the body of Christ. Today, as in the first centuries of Christianity when the Johannine author wrote, the temptation to deny our bodiliness and thus deny the Body of Christ persists. Worship is not only a time when our souls are saved. Worship is a total experience in which God wishes to be most intimate with us, to touch our feelings, our hearts, our emotions, our bodies, the depths of our being.

Though reasoned statements about God can be used in worship, scripture in its use of poetry and story seems to imply that art forms with their element of beauty and mystery beyond reason are better forms to communicate a God who is beauty and mystery beyond reason. Music, poetry, mime, dance, and drama are ways that can help us experience the transforming power of the words of the eucharistic prayers and the gestures of taking, blessing, breaking, and sharing the bread. The history of salvation, Isaiah's hymn which sings "Holy, Holy, Holy..." congregational responses within the prayer, Jesus' gestures at the Last Supper, the memorial acclamation, the invocation of the Holy Spirit, the rememberance of all the Church, and the sharing of

Christ's life through bread and wine are all elements which have rich possibilities for dance interpretation. Because these parts are so important in Christian worship, they invite our best arts for emphasis. Though prose words of our prayers can convey something about God's activity and our response of thanks and praise, the use of the arts to explicate the prose opens our hearts to God. One glimpse of creation reveals that God is a dancer, an artist, and a poet. When we use not only the minimal prayers and the minimal gestures in our worship, but try to make worship creative and beautiful, we are cooperating with God. The Spirit can move in places in our selves where we are fearful, bound, and inhibited. The Spirit brings healing and wholeness.

In Christian tradition there are strong precedents for using dance in eucharistic worship. Whether explicit theology of the human body as a symbol of the Body of Christ or spontaneous devotion, which so

often reveals the Spirit speaking directly to the hearts of the faithful, or both motivated dance in the Spanish church is not known, but dance has been used extensively. Even in the Middle Ages, when an impoverished theology of the eucharist led persons to focus on merely looking at the consecrated bread as a means of contacting Christ rather than taking and eating as He commanded, dance was done to celebrate the eucharistic Body of Christ. There has been a rich tradition of dance before the Blessed Sacrament both in churches and in procession. Today, as we better understand the eucharist as the dynamic action of Christ, not merely His static presence in the bread and wine, our dances should reflect this. As dance has been used in all Christian centuries to reveal the mystery of Christ, so dance can be used to enflesh the insights of contemporary eucharistic theology.

The Bishops' Committee on the Liturgy calls for quality and appropriateness in the atmosphere and environment for worship and applies this to "music, architecture, sculpture, painting, pottery making, furniture making, as well as to dance, mime or drama — in other words, to any art form that might be employed in the liturgical environment or action."[2] When using the dances described in this text or any others, they should be measured against the criteria for quality given: "Quality means love and care in the making of something, honesty and genuineness in the use of materials, and the artist's special gift in producing an harmonious whole."[3] Are our dances made with love and care, honesty and genuineness, and are they harmonious as wholes? The quest for quality in religious arts is not an easy one. Neither hasty work on an art form, nor hasty decisions by spectators about its quality can be used. Both artist and observer must listen with the ears of the heart and see with the eyes of the heart to identify quality. "Quality is perceived only by contemplation, by standing back from things and really trying to see them, trying to let them speak to the beholder."[4] If a community at first would not see the meaning or beauty in dance, could the fault be not with the dance but with the fact that our society has not taught us to contemplate? Too often we live in words of the pragmatic, rushed, and rational. Religion has been sandwiched into this as a pragmatic means of welfare in the afterlife, but authentic religion should shatter those worlds and give us the ability to live in a completely different dimension, a contemplative dimension. Arts in the Church both spring from contemplation and lead to contemplation.

An art used in worship should not only be of quality, but also be appropriate. Appropriateness means that: "1) it must be capable of bearing the weight of mystery, awe, reverence, and wonder which the liturgical action expresses; 2) it must clearly serve (and not interrupt) ritual action which has its own structure, rhythm and movement."[5] For the arts to serve and not interrupt the ritual action, attention needs to be paid to which ritual actions of the liturgy are of greater and of lesser importance. The arts should focus on and not distract from the dynamics of ritual.

This text has explained that the proclamation of the Word of God and the eucharistic prayers and actions are high points of Christian worship. It is appropriate to emphasize and beautify them whether this be in word, music, drama, audio visuals, or dance. Other parts of worship which are of lesser importance need to be critically studied by liturgist and by artist and evaluated in relation to the whole. For example, the location, meaning, and importance of the penitential rite in the current Catholic eucharist liturgy is questionable. The service begins with an invitation to pray and often with a song, a welcome, or acknowledgement of our gracious God who has gathered us. While God's word and holiness challenge our world and us personally to greater goodness, it is questionable whether a reflection on personal sinfulness at this point is appropriate in the flow of the ritual. Dance can be a most effective way of expressing confession and reconciliation, but such dance should be done at appropriate times in the dynamics of a service or only in services particularly focusing on repentance.

The Lamb of God was added to the eucharistic liturgy of the Roman rite in the sixth century as a background hymn during the important gesture of breaking the consecrated bread, one of the four major actions of the eucharistic service (taking, blessing, breaking, and sharing bread). The Lamb of God should only be danced if the movement focuses in some way on the central gesture of breaking the bread or is a response to it. Because any part of worship could be danced, mimed, or dramatized, as any part could be sung, that does not mean it should be. As a good director of a play knows the high points in a drama, the points of lesser significance, and the transitions, so the liturgical artists should understand the dynamics of the whole liturgy. Contemporary artists and theologians, as those who built and decorated Gothic cathedrals, must stay in dialogue: the artists to be rooted in sound principles, and the theologians to have their imaginations stimulated that they may soar to the heights.

This chapter describes some of the traditional movements, dances, or themes of Mexican and Native American peoples which could contribute to contemporary Christianity. This text is not a detailed history, anthropology, or record of choreography, but a collection of ideas that can be springboards to creativity. The brief historical notes hopefully will lead readers to a more thorough study of the rich cultures of these peoples. The music, costumes, and movements are to stimulate artistic imagination. Whether the following dances are used in education or worship, it is important that there be previous introduction and preparation for them, and that they be integrated into the whole. Repetition or elaboration of a theme, music, or gesture both clarify and deepen their meaning. Finally, and most importantly, these dances are meant to be enjoyed.

Processions and Pilgrimages

The most common types of movements used in Mexican and Native American communities have been processions and pilgrimages. While some contemporary spirituality has tended to discredit such popular piety, the history of processions and pilgrimages in the Judeo-Christian tradition affirms their value. The technical theological term for describing the activity of the Trinity is "procession." Christ the Son proceeds from the Creator. Christians of the West have described the Spirit as proceeding from the Creator and the Son, while Christians of the East have said that the Spirit proceeds from the Creator alone. These descriptions are about a God who is immaterial, and yet movement words, dance words, seem to be the best way to describe God's involvement and loving activity. The Hebrew people would go in joyful procession up to Jerusalem, and many of the psalms celebrate this movement.

A pilgrimage involves a spiritual commitment. One leaves the comforts of home, the companionship of friends and family. One leaves one's security and travels in faith to another place. As persons might go away on retreat to separate themselves from everyday activity in order to more fully concentrate on God, so persons go on pilgrimages. Abraham and Sarah were invited to leave security and to go wherever God would lead them. Led by Moses, Aaron, and Miriam, the Israelites in Egypt were invited to leave their security. Paul's missionary travels could be described as pilgrimages. During the Middle Ages pilgrimages became very popular, as Chaucer's *Canterbury Tales* reveal. Though the brutality of the crusades could be questioned today, the idea behind them was to make the Holy Land accessible for those who felt called to go on pilgrimage there to pray at the holy places. As well as being interested in the places where Christ lived, persons would also go to places where saints lived, were buried, or were remembered. The apostle James is supposedly buried at the shrine in Santiago di Compostela. This town in northern Spain became one of the most popular places of pilgrimage. Hotels for travelers and many churches grew up along the roads across Europe that led to it.

The Spaniards brought the spirituality of pilgrimages with them to the New World. The most popular place of pilgrimage in Mexico today is the shrine of Our lady of Guadalupe in Mexico City. This is probably because it commemorates the Christian God's concern for the indigenous people of America. As in the beginning of Luke's gospel the appearance of Mary points to the appearance of Christ, so she appeared as a Native American maiden and spoke in Nahuatl, their language. She heralded not a distant God of the foreign invaders, but a universal God who blesses all the peoples of the earth and who is imaged by red, brown, black, yellow, and white people.

Other popular places of pilgrimage in Mexico are Chalma and Los Remedios. San Juan is popular in Texas, and Chimayo in New Mexico. A pilgrimage can be a type of moving meditation helping one to lay aside daily problems and to focus on the endpoint where God is to be encountered in a special way. All earthly pilgrimages are only partial, but call attention to the final goal, the heavenly city, the New Jerusalem, and complete union with God.

Processions can be a type of pilgrimage. Circle dances have been popular in religious rites through the ages, and have been used in

Jewish and Christian worship; but processional dance more clearly expresses the Judeo-Christian world view. In this tradition, God's intervention in history is experienced in linear time, rather than in cyclical time as is taught in many Eastern religions. Early Christians would move in procession through the streets and into the church to celebrate the Sunday and special feasts. Processions not only focused on drawing Christians into a sanctuary and closer to each other, but they also indicated God's peace and blessing going out to the village, the fields, the shops, the homes — that is, to the whole secular world.

Persons today might timidly have a procession from the front steps of the church into the sanctuary, drawing in spiritual energy, but would they dare to have a procession, a parade, through the main street of town and "go public," witnessing that they believe in a God who permeates life all week, not just one with whom we seclude ourselves on Sundays? If a church community had a public procession like this, they might begin to feel the need to help improve the neighborhood. A procession outward is turning a church inside out. A procession is taking Pentecost seriously. The followers of Jesus huddled together and hid in the upper room. The Spirit would not let them remain isolated: they were sent out to the ends of the earth. Many persons would feel uncomfortable with a religious procession that goes into the outside world because they would rather keep their religion isolated from life.

Pre-Christian religions would often have processions out into the fields at the time of planting, to beseech the spirits to make the earth fertile. In Christianity the rogation days were set aside as special times in which the priests and people would go forth to the land, praying and singing along the way and asking God's blessing. Such actions may remind God to intervene, but they also have a salutary effect of reminding all in the community that they are called to participate in God's work of creation, to tend the garden God made with care and diligence. The earth is like the vineyard spoken of in the gospel, entrusted to people while the master is away. We are to be faithful stewards. It will be our children's children who will suffer if we are not. Marches for justice led by Martin Luther King, Jr. and Cesar Chavez, the Long Walk of the Native Americans, and marches for peace and human rights have shown how processions continue to be meaningful. Like the three processions around the city of Jericho in the book of Judges, this community movement can break down walls with the help of God.

Las Posadas

One popular form of religious procession of the Christmas season is Las Posadas, which commemorates Mary and Joseph seeking lodging. The practice was developed by the Franciscan missionaries in Mexico in 1587 to offset a revival of celebrations to honor the Aztec god of war. Traditionally, for nine nights before Christmas persons walk in procession with candles, singing and praying. They either carry statues of Mary and Joseph, or have two persons dressed as them. They knock at different places; using the traditional songs, they ask for shelter, but are refused. Prayers that we may learn to welcome the needy, aliens, unwed mothers, persons of a different sexual orientation, strangers — all these might be appropriate. Finally at the last place Mary and Joseph are welcomed, enter, pray and have a fiesta, a party.

In Posada fiestas traditional Mexican folk dancing is popular. The delightful suggestions for involving everyone in Christmas carols through dancing as well as singing in the book, *Dancing Christmas Carols,* could be used, Beating on a piñata, which may be a symbol of the devil, is one of the favorite games in the celebration. In New Mexico the piñata is often a star shape, called the star of Bethlehem. When it is broken, blessings of candy, nuts, and toys spill forth. In Las Posadas the authentic Spanish songs or other familiar carols and prayers may be used. Traditional words and music for Las Posada can be found in *A Treasury of Mexican Folkways,* or in the booklet and cassette made by the Mexican American Cultural Center. (The sources and descriptions of these and of other resources mentioned in the text are given at the end of this book.)

Los Pastores: The Shepherds

During the Christmas season an ancient play about the shepherds is popular in Mexico and parts of the southwestern United States. The origin of this mystery play is attributed to Lope de Vega, the medieval Spanish dramatist. Franciscan missionaries brought it to Mexico in the early 1500's as a means of teaching the native peoples. Rarely were the text and music written down. Rather, they were memorized and passed from generation to generation. Today the Museum of New Mexico in Santa Fe has fourteen variations of the play. All have the same basic characters and story. Besides Mary and Joseph, the Magi and shepherds, there are Michael with his loyal followers, Lucifer and his seven devils signifying the seven deadly sings, the holy hermits who urge on the shepherds, and a jester. The masked demons with

each of their enticements try to stop the shepherds along the way. This is really a pilgrimage of life. The dialogue is humorous, but leads to some poignant moments. The costumes used are interesting examples of indigenization. Shepherds in south Texas wear straw cowboy hats, while those in New Mexico wear sombreros!

Much of Los Pastores can be done in song and dance. The Matachines dances are often held before the play, with a fiesta with Mariachis, as well as many folk dances for the Christ child at the end. The play often includes the Danza de las Pastorcitas a joyful dance of little shepherd girls in elaborate dresses and hats decked with flowers and ribbons. Sometimes the combat of Michael and the archangels against Lucifer and the devils is done in the form of a dance called Los Migueles. There is much laughter when the forces of evil are overthrown and the devils go sprawling and kicking on the ground. The dance of the Ermitanos, the holy old hermits in pointed hoods or hats who try to lead the shepherds to the Child, is a procession in which the hermits put their hands on the shoulders of the one in front and move together.

An Argentinian musical version of a folk drama based on the nativity is available on the album *Misa Criolla*. Both the drama and the mass on this album are excellent for dancing. The warmly human and humorous folk songs include types of music from different regions. There are songs about the Annunciation, the pilgrimage of Joseph and Mary to Bethlehem, Christ's birth, the coming of the shepherds and of the three kings, and the holy family's flight to Egypt. The flowers, plants, and the land of America give rich imagery in the poetry, as the rhythms of America shape the music. The work of art is a truly incarnational expression of God's beaty in a particular place and time, and invites a response of dance.

Matachines

One of the most widespread Mexican dances is that of the Matachines. As has been mentioned, the Spanish missionaries brought the term to the New World; it is often associated with the Moors who were in Spain for so many centuries. The missionaries may have taught the natives a new dance, but it seems more likely that the simple step was already part of the Native American religious ritual. In the form of Matachines dances done in New Mexico, there is a symbolic drama which perhaps was originally associated with characters in the medieval morality plays, but the interaction is not clearly defined today. There is usually a pretty young girl dressed in white dress and veil as for first communion. There is a king or leader, a clown with a whip, and a devil clown. The dancers wear tall head-dresses like bishops' mitres, and their faces are covered with cloth. They carry three-pronged sticks in one hand and rattles in the other. At times the devil dances on all fours and the king symbolically puts his foot on the subject creature.

In Mexico the term Matachines is used more broadly to mean a devotional dance done with simple steps. On a special feast the dance might be done from the natives' residences in the mountains all the way down to the village. The dance might be done for one day or for several, as an intense and concentrated form of prayer. The emphasis is not on performance for spectators, but on the interior prayerfulness of the dancer. The dancers can move alone, in rows, or move in patterns of two rows doing arrangements something like the grand march.

The basic step is usually done to very repetitious violin music with a regular beat. The basic step involves sliding the right foot along the ground, then stepping firmly on it, then sliding the left foot and stepping firmly on it. The earth is sacred, a gift of God, and this dance is one of firmly contacting the earth in prayer. The arms have no particular movement, though one may carry a rattle or improvise arm movements. The head is bent slightly forward. One does not gaze at others around, but rather turns one's vision inward toward God.

In many religious traditions there are forms of meditation that involve a simple repetitious movement. Dervishes, a group of ascetic Moslems, are known for their whirling dances. Sufis have many types of dances with repeated movements. In Hasidism, a mystical sect of Judaism, swaying, chanting, and moving have been recognized as ways of freeing the mind for deep union with God. When a person gets caught up in a particular bodily movement, it slowly draws together the thoughts and energy. The multiple distractions and tensions in one's life begin to be left aside. One begins to do just one thing at a time, and this helps integrate one's personality and opens one to God.

The Matachines dance could be done by a small group for the rest of the congregation, but ideally, all should be invited to do it as a

personal meditation. It could begin some distance from the church or could be done around the church. Authentic Matachines music is not always available, but the simple slide step can easily be done to other native American music with regular beat. The Gloria from "Rosas del Tepayac" by Carlos Rosas is based on Aztec music and can be used effectively for Matachines processions around or into the church. Such music and dance as a general praise of God would be appropriate at any special service.

The basic step could also be used to *Danze Azteca, Los Quetzales,* and *Danza de los Sonajeros* selections on the album of the *Ballet Folklorico.*

La Llorona: The Weeping Woman

La Llorona, which means the wailing woman, is a plaintive melody from the Mexican region of Tehuantepec, based on a popular folk legend. It tells of a mysterious woman who is heard wailing in the night. Who is she? Why does she cry? Has she lost a child? Has she lost a lover? The text of the song implies that the one who has heard La Llorona and tried to get a glimpse of her is one who has lost a beloved. The words say: "One who loves, suffers."

The dance is often done by low light with a woman or women in long dark dresses with veils (the lacy black mantillas traditionally worn to church) who move slowly and mournfully but lightly as spirits. The dancer can hold her full skirt and move it in large graceful gestures occasionally. If there is a group of dancers, they can hold hands in the center and circle in a star pattern, then move away into dark isolation. The dancer has the ambiguous quality of a mysterious figure in the night who attracts one, yet frightens one away. Such ambiguity is often characteristic of one who is grieving. When someone has lost a child or is in danger of death, we want to sympathetically stand by and respond, but at the same time we fear doing so. Being near one grieving is being vulnerable. It is opening up to grief as well. Jesus is the ultimate example of one who was willing to become vulnerable. In his Incarnation he entered the world in which suffering existed and was willing to accept it. The dance of La Llorona, which shows that "one who loves, suffers," can reflect the experience of Jesus.

The music of *La Llorona* is on the record *Ballet Folklorico,* or the music and text may be found in the book *A Treasury of Mexican Folkways.*

La Llorona could be used in educational programs on coping with grief or death. The dance could be associated with those who suffer after the losses of war or a natural disaster. In worship La Llorona could be associated with the paschal mystery which finds life despite death. The following scriptural texts could be used with the dance. Rachel, the mother of the nation Israel, lamented that most of her children had been killed in the destruction of Jerusalem or had been carried off to Babylonian concentration camps in Ramah: "In Ramah is heard the sound of moaning, of bitter weeping! Rachel mourns her children, she refuses to be consoled because her children are no more" (Jeremiah 31:15).

The woman of Jerusalem lamented over the suffering of Christ. Jesus said to them: "Daughters of Jerusalem, do not weep for me. Weep for yourselves and for your children" (Luke 23:28).

Mary stood grieving as she watched Christ die (see John 19:25).

Los Concheros
Conchero dancing which goes back to prehispanic times is still practiced by thousands of men and women in Mexico, especially in Guanajuato, Queretaro, Tlaxcala, Hidalgo, and the Federal District. Being a Conchero is not just participating in a dance, but means being part of a religious group that involves an initiation ceremony of ritual, prayer, and promises to be a faithful soldier of Christ. Being faithful means helping other members of the group in times of sickness or death, forgiving and making up differences if one has quarreled, and helping each other on the pilgrimages to the holy places. Also, a Conchero promises to treat everyone with respect and consideration.

Each group is led by a captain who may be a woman or a man. They meet regularly to practice dances, but even this is considered real prayer. The dance is never mere exercise or display.

The Concheros have particular devotion to Christ and to Mary as they are honored at four sanctuaries that are considered to mark the

69

four directions (from Mexico City): La Villa de Guadalupe (north); Chalma (south); Los Remedios (west), and Amecameca (east). The four directions, in the shape of a cross, is central in the form of their dances. The cross was important in prehispanic times because the people believed that good energies came from all four directions and should be integrated in the center. The Concheros also recount a story of why they use the cross. During the last battle between the Spanish and the Chichemecas, which took place near Queretaro on July 25, 1531, a shining cross appeared in the sky beside St. James, the patron of Spain. The native peoples saw the sign, became peaceful, and wanted to accept the new religion which was signified by the cross. This story is similar to the explanation of how the Roman Empire came to accept Christianity. Constantine saw a cross in the sky and took it as a sign that he was called to conversion. The Chichemecas wished a permanent cross to be placed there and they celebrated their new faith in dance.

Traditionally a Conchero group has a "devil" who wears a wild mask and carries a whip. The devil clears a way for the rest of the dancers through the people, cracks his whip, performs antics, keeps the spectators from crowding, and generally adds comic relief while these dances of cosmic harmony are being done. The dances were considered so important and sacred in the past that one who did not do them properly could be punished by beating or death, because the dances pertained to the harmony of the cosmos. Yet, a clown danced among them.

Usually the Conchero dances are done in front of the church, but they begin on the inside. The dancers stand in front of the altar, bow, and pray; then they back out, still facing the altar as a sign that they are continuing to focus on God. Before and after going into the church the dancers form a figure, face each of the four directions, and pray, asking for a pure intention. They then walk in two lines and form a circle around a fire which symbolizes the sun. Often incense is used. The leader begins the dance by uttering a loud call and tracing the sign of the cross on the ground with his or her foot. Some of the Concheros play music. Though banjos and mandolins may be used, the most common instrument, and that from which the dance takes its name, is the concho, a stringed instrument made of an armadillo shell. The dancers represent the movement of the planets around the sun and their dance is a prayer that things may move in harmony in the cosmos. The dance is light and graceful, with nimble springs. The dancers hop on one foot while making a cross in the air with the other. They cross their feet and rock from side to side. They go down on one knee like a genuflection, and also jump up, raising each knee high. The music begins slowly, but increases in volume and speed until it reaches climax. The dance then suddenly stops.

The adornments that are most typical of the Concheros are elaborate headdresses with long waving feathers. Some may have mirrors or beadwork. Each dancer is different: the women let their hair hang loose and wear brightly colored dresses, while the men wear a variety of things from skirts with beads to leather suits to long satin capes with only breechcloths underneath. The Concheros often carry banners with images of Christ or the saints. These are decorated with ribbons. *Musica Prehispanic Y Mestiza de Mexico* contains

songs played and sung by Conchero groups. Ideally Concheros should provide their own music on mandolin, concho, or banjo.

Concheros traditionally dance on many feasts of the liturgical year. The feast of the Holy Cross which is important in Mexico is often celebrated in dance. Saint Augustine and other early theologians wrote of the cross not merely as an instrument of torture, but as a symbol of God's love which in its shape reaches out in all directions to touch the whole cosmos. They associated the shape of the cross with the hymn extolling God's limitless love in Ephesians 3. The cross implies "the breadth, the length, the height, and the depth" of the love of Christ (Ephesians 3:18). The cross patterns in Conchero dances and the associations with all the cosmos can re-echo the message of Ephesians that divine love completely encompasses us and that God's "power working in us can do infinitely more than we ask or imagine" (Ephesians 3:20). In Conchero and other dances which grow in enthusiasm and speed until one seems to be carried by a power beyond oneself, there is a sense of ecstatic release. This release hints at the mystical insight of Ephesians that God's power can carry us beyond ourselves, even beyond the limits of our imaginations.

Dance of the Four Directions

Most religions in one way or another incorporate ideas about the four directions in their symbols or rituals. A prayer used on the Jewish feast of Sukkot, a time of thanking God for the bountiful harvest, includes facing in each direction as a *lulav*, a ritual object made of palm, is waved. This symbolizes taking in God's peace from every direction. Many Jewish homes have a *mizrah*, a special plaque or picture on the east wall to orient them towards Jerusalem and thus symbolically to focus their attention on praising God in all of life. Christian churches have traditionally been build on an east-west axis so that the rising sun would shine in over the altar to remind worshippers of Christ the Dawning Light. Native American tepees and houses traditionally have the door on the east side to let in the first light of the sun. Navajo sand paintings used in curing rituals have a cross on the ground pointing out the cardinal directions. Many Native American dances, as the Conchero dance, involve a pattern of facing the cardinal directions. The following is a simple adaptation of orientation dances that has been used successfully in both small groups and larger congregations. It invites meditation and movement.

The leader invites all to reflect on the importance of orientation in their lives. What happens if you rearrange the furniture in your home and forget about it when you wake up in the middle of the night? What happens if you take a north rather than a south turn on the freeway? How do we become disoriented? How is emotional or psychic disorientation even more difficult than physical? At times when you have been disoriented, what has helped you? What does it mean to orient one's life towards God?

The leader should explain how the whole movement meditation will be done. The leader invites persons to call out names, things, feelings, or just words that they associate with north. Then people are invited to mention things associated with east, south, and west. The leader might want to write them down. Then the leader invites the group to face in each direction as she or he will say a prayer improvised from their suggestions. The persons are invited to stand breathing in the air of that direction with hands held low and palms open. As the leader finishes the prayer of each direction with the words "Thank you God for the north (east,south, west) and all the experiences the north (east, south, west) brings to me," persons reach up with palms still open as if receiving the good power of that direction and pulling it down over their faces and bodies.

The following are prayers that emerged from the words suggested by one group. It is, however, important to let each group speak of its own experiences: (Facing north) "Oh God of the north, we meet you in challenge and cold winds. We open ourselves to darkness, ... ice, ... crisp, clear air, ... winter, ... Santa Claus. Thank you God for the north and all the experiences that the north brings to me."

(Facing east) "Oh God of the east, we know you in the rising sun; you are the dawn of justice. We open ourselves to freshness, ... the source, ... germination, ... fund, ... the orient, ... spring. Thank you God for the east and all the experiences the east brings to me."

(Facing south) "Oh God of the south, we know you in gentle breezes and brownskins. We open ourselves to warmth, ... dryness, ... flowers, ... a relaxed tempo, ... summer. Thank you God for the south and all the experiences the south brings me.

(Facing west) "Oh God of the west, we know you as our fulfillment and end. We open ourselves to rest, ... peace, ... sunset, ... lingering moments, ... fall, ... the harvest. Thank you God for the west and all the experiences the west brings to me."

At the end people can close their eyes and give thanks to the God above them, the God below them, and the God within them.

Las Canacuas

Las Canacuas is a ritual of hospitality done by the Tarascans. The indigenous name of the people is "those who visit," or Purépecha. The ritual through dance shows the welcome given to strangers and all who visit. Mexico has many varieties of hospitality dances. Guelaguetza means offering and is the name given to a dance done by the Zapotecs to welcome visitors and show respect to their governors. One of the most impressive welcomes is the Feather dance, which takes very skilled dancers to do the intricate movements while wearing large elaborate feather headdresses. In Oaxaca, jarapes, dances with light and lyrical steps, are the typical ritual of hospitality.

The Tarascan dancers wear full black skirts, white blouses with embroidered flowers, and white aprons decorated with trim. They carry on their heads large lacquer trays with painted designs which are filled with fruits and flowers. Baskets could be used if lacquer trays are not available. The whole dance is done very lightly and the dancers smile and look at each guest to reinforce their gestures of hospitality. The music for Las Canacuas and detailed instructions for the dance are included in the book *Regional Dances of Mexico* and a cassette of the music in that book is also available. Other light lyrical music from the south of Mexico would also be appropriate, such as the selections from Veracruz or Tehuantepec on the *Ballet Folklorico de Mexico* album.

Dancers enter from both sides, taking small steps to the beat of the music. They cross each other, then form lines facing each other. They dance forward and backward, turn around, still using small steps. One woman stands in the middle holding her tray up while the others circle her. They kneel, holding their trays toward her. The trays are put on the floor and the dancers circle them. Parts of this can be varied and repeated until the main part of the dance ritual, in which the women gracefully move among the guests. The women give them fruit and throw the flowers into the air. All that they have should be given away, as a sign of their total graciousness, and as the music ends the dancers should gather in a symmetrical formation holding the trays and displaying their lovely designs.

In education or worship this dance could be used in association with scriptural texts on hospitality. Hospitality was a very important virtue in the biblical world. The difficulty of travel and the dangers of the desert reinforced this idea which is illustrated in stories of Lot's duty to care for his guests (see Genesis 19) and Laban and Rebekah's welcome to Isaac (see Genesis 24). Abraham and Sarah welcomed three strangers, and in doing so, invited the presence of God, which blessed Abraham and the aged Sarah with a son (see Genesis 18). Persons who opened their homes and their hearts to guests also opened themselves to receive God's ever faithful love.

The parable of the Good Samaritan is an invitation to hospitality towards rather than neglect of the strangers we encounter (see Luke 10:25-37). Saint Paul urges the early Christian community to "be generous in offering hospitality" (Romans 12:13). The first letter of Peter directs: "Be mutually hospitable without complaining. As generous distributors of God's manifold grace, put your gifts at the service of one another, each in the measure that he has received" (I Peter 4:9-10). The letter to the Hebrews recommends: "Remember always to welcome strangers, for by doing this, some people have entertained angels without knowing it" (Hebrews 13:2).

God is likened to a guest who stands at the door and knocks. If it is opened, God will come in. It is not so much the guest who is blessed by the hospitality, but rather the host: "Anyone who loves me will be true to my word, and my Father will love him; we will come to him and make our dwelling place with him" (John 14:23). Christ washed the feet of his apostles, the eastern gesture of hospitality toward guests. John's gospel records this gesture and not the breaking and sharing of bread which is described by the other evangelists. Both these actions from which come our eucharistic rituals seem to have a similar meaning of reaching out in love and service toward the other. How is the eucharist a dance of hospitality? How can the Canacuas ritual of sharing fruit and flowers help us to understand our communion with bread and wine?

El Venado: The Deer

This version of a Deer dance, a theme common to many Native American groups, is from the Yaqui group of northern Mexico and Arizona. It is the story of a graceful, powerful stag who ultimately provides nourishment for the people. The dance essentially pantomimes a handsome deer moving through the forest and delighting in life. Observation of a deer is the best preparation for the dancer. The dancer wears close-fitting tan garments and an antler headdress. Music for this can be found in *A Treasury of Mexican Folkways,* but a simple drum rhythm can be most effective. The Yaqui use drum, flute, and rattles. A hunter with stylized movements shoots the deer. The wounded animal goes through a mime of pain and gradually diminishing strength, until death.

Religious rituals involve symbols which are open to many associations and meanings. They do not have a one-to-one correspondence as signs do. This dance begins by expressing great vitality. Then, it reveals suffering and death which are evil but can be endured with beauty as in this dance form. The death brings nourishment and life to others. This dance could be done in association with scripture readings on Christ who lived fully, endured suffering with love rather than bitterness, and gave his flesh for the life of the world. As has been mentioned in the chapter on Native American spiritualities and ecology, a person who would wish to use a part of nature — whether it be a tree, water, an animal, or something else — would ask the spirit of that thing if it would sacrifice itself for the good of the other. Christ was willing to lay down His life for His friends.

El Venado could be used with the suffering servant songs of Isaiah, where the prophet describes one who suffers for the good of others. Christianity has applied the passages to Christ. These passages include Isaiah 42:1-2; 49:1-6; 50:4-11; and 52:13-53b.

Similarly, the narratives of Christ's last supper with his friends speak of giving his body and blood for the forgiveness of sins and for the life of the world (see Matthew 26:26-28; Mark 14:22-24; Luke 22:14-20).

La Tortuga: The Turtle

A lovely melody that is played on the marimba and comes from the Mexican region of Tehuantepec is La Tortuga, the Turtle. The music and dance are associated with the spring and with fertility. At times Christianity has shied away from anything that might be associated with sexuality, but this is cutting persons off from the rich symbolic imagery of scripture which reveals the God of life in the glory of created life processes. Scripture, in fact, begins with the command to be fruitful and to multiply. God's relationship with persons is imaged in the faithful love between man and woman, alluded to by Isaiah, Jeremiah, and Ezechiel. The Song of Songs is a series of love poems. They may originally have been written to express the beauty of human love, but they came to be used in scripture to describe the joys of divine love. Throughout history dance has been associated with love, whether this be love between persons or love between persons and the divine. Lovers have a sense of their hearts dancing within them and soon their whole selves join in this rhythm.

The traditional costumes of Tehuantepec are long full white skirts with shorter black skirts over them with rich embroidery of nature. On their heads women wear a white circular ruffled cloth that almost covers their hair completely. They carry large baskets of flowers. The music of La Tortuga is in *A Treasury of Mexican Folkways*. Other suitable popular songs can be found on the album *Ballet Folklorico*. The dance involves moving along in a step-together-step rhythm while gracefully circling the basket of flowers. There is a graceful twisting of the hips and the body that affirms that all of our body, not just that part from the waist up, has been made by God and should be celebrated. Traditionally the dance is done with women standing in straight lines and moving and swaying in unison, creating a lovely pattern with their skirts and headdresses.

La Tortuga could be used with readings from the Song of Songs, describing the beauty of love, of spring, and of life. Psalms or parts of Job celebrating the beauty and goodness of God's created world could also be used (see Psalms 24, 45, 65, 67, 104; Job 30-41). The dance could be used in a wedding celebration or spring festival.

Alleluia

Dancing the proclamation of Alleluia before the reading of the gospel, the good news, is one of the most appropriate times for movement.

This is a simple dance done with the song "Aleluya" of the mass "Rosas de Tepeyac." The text of the verses speaks of Our Lady of Guadalupe and could be used the year around. This dance could be adapted to almost any Alleluia verse or hymn focusing on the Word of

God; Mexican or Native American costumes could be used. The main dancer holds the book out of which the scripture is to be read. This book should be made of fine quality materials and embellished in such a way as to indicate its importance. Each dancer carries a flower, a palm branch, a candle, and incense — that is, something lovely to surround the scriptures. In India, in the Roman Catholic rite involving indigenous customs that have been approved for national use, the scripture book may be surrounded by a circle of flowers before it is read, to draw attention to the importance of the Word of God.

The main dancer moves toward the place where the scripture will be read, holding up the book and gracefully dancing with it. The other

dancers surround the main dancer, moving rhythmically and focusing attention on the book. During verse one they sway in and out toward the main dancer, raising their flowers, incense, or candles. During the next chorus and verse two, they circle the scriptures, indicating that it is God's word which centers and draws us. All move forward during the chorus, and as the book is placed on its stand in verse three, dancers reach toward it. During the final chorus each places his or her ceremonial object in an attractive arrangement around the book and then stands in an attentive way nearby to listen to the reading of scripture. The reverence and attention of the dancers can lead the congregation to attentive posture and mood.

Praise of Creation

Though this text has concentrated on Native American contact with Hispanic Christianity, it seems desirable to include a lovely Native American hymn that is easily accessible: "Many and Great, O God." The text and music can be found in *The Methodist Hymnal* (Nashville: Methodist Publishing House, 1966). It is most effective when done with voice and drum.

During an introduction of only drum beats, the dancer or dancers begin simply stepping to the regular beat of the drum. This basic rhythmic slow movement of the feet continues throughout the dance. The dancer uses slow stylized mime movements suggesting the parts

of creation which are described: earth, stars, mountains, and waters. If a group of dancers does this, the communion with God described in the second verse can be implied by circling and being in relationship with each other.

Many and Great, O God

American Folk Hymn   LACQUIPARLE, irregular
Paraphrased by Philip Frazier,
1892-1964
from the *Dakota Indian Hymnal*

> Many and great, O God, are thy things,
> Maker of earth and sky;
> Thy hands have set the heavens with stars;
> Thy fingers spread the mountains and plains.
> Lo, at thy word the waters were formed;
> Deep seas obey thy voice.
>
> Grant unto us communion with thee,
> Thou star abiding one;
> Come unto us and dwell with us;
> With thee are found the gifts of life.
> Bless us with life that has no end,
> Eternal life with thee. Amen.

This song praising God for creation is appropriate throughout the year, but it could be used especially for Thanksgiving, services focusing on ecology, or on the day the Catholic Church commemorates Blessed Kateri Tekawitha. After being ostracized by her family for becoming a Christian, she fled about 200 miles through the wilderness to live in a Christian Native American village near Montreal. She is known for her care for others and prayerfulness, and has come to be called the Lily of the Mohawks.

Los Viejitos: The Little Old Men

One of the most popular humorous dances in Mexico had its very ancient origins in prehispanic times. Friar Diego Duran, in his *Historia de las Indias de la Nueva España* wrote of the dance of the little old men in which they wore masks with wrinkled faces. They danced with great charm and brought much laughter. They were associated with the ancient god Huehueteotl, the spirit of fire and old age who is so often depicted in pre-columbian ceramics as a wrinkled old man with a warm smile. He seems like the wise and kind grandfather by the home fire. The dance is best preserved in the state of Michoacán, particularly in the region of Lake Pátzcuaro. The people of the sierra of Uruapan tell the history of the birth of Christ: that persons from all parts of the world came to worship him and give him rich gifts. The little old men had no wealth to give the Christ child, so they offered him the abundance of their long lives expressed in dance. When they danced, Christ was so pleased that he smiled at them. The dance is used every Christmas in his way, but is done at other times of the year as well. Since the old men were once associated with the god of fire, this dance may express that the many gods reverenced by the natives came to worship the one Christian God.

The dancers wear white shirts and pants with colorful bandanas around their necks. Short striped sarapes may be worn. Wrinkled benevolent masks with white hair and crooked canes upon which the dancers lean give the dance its particular humorous flavor. While flat-brimmed straw sombreros decorated with ribbons and fringe are used in most places, the people of the mountains around Uruapan, Michoacán, wear no hats but large funny wigs made of straw.

The dance is done to a rhythmic lively beat. The dancers hobble and do the whole dance bent over, leaning on their canes. Throughout the dance they make amusing mime gestures of holding their aching backs, expressing weariness, and almost tripping, yet they continue and delight in the dancing. The leader taps his cane three times as a signal to begin, and the dancers repeat the taps to show they are ready. The main movement of the dance is a zapateado done in place, which consists of stepping right, left, right, left, right. Between the zapateado different variations can be done. Little jumps like a game of hopscotch are repeated. Often the dancers land with feet and knees apart and shake as they try to steady themselves on their canes. They hop, landing with right toe behind the left foot and then the opposite. They hop around following the leader. They can balance on their toes and click their heels together. The dancers face each other in two lines, go forward and back, then swing head and shoulders. In festivals, this dance is often continued all day long, with the leader tapping and giving gestures of which pattern to follow.

The music and dance directions for Los Viejitos are included in *Regional Dances of Mexico,* and a cassette of the music is also available. The dance could also be done to almost any zapateado or jarape music. Some are included in the record *Ballet Folklorico de Mexico.*

Traditionally, Mexicans have had a deep respect for the elderly, which they promote through family intergenerational gatherings. This is not a dance laughing at the elderly, but rather, a dance laughing with them as they express their joy in life through dance, though their backs are bent and their joints are wobbly. They know God's promise: "Even to your old age I am the same, even when your hair is gray I will bear you " (Isaiah 46:4). The prophets often described the agility of the weak as a sign of the reign of God. God "will save the lame" (Zephaniah 3:19). "Strengthen all weary hands, steady all trembling knees and say to all faint hearts, 'Courage! Do not be afraid. Look, your God is coming.'... Then the lame shall leap like deer" (Isaiah 35:3-4, 6).

This dance could be used for intergenerational discussions in a church. What perspectives can age bring? How can these lead one to "dance" in the face of many situations that earlier in life might have brought a paralyzing fear? The aged Simeon and Anna had the ability to recognize a baby in the temple as the Christ while most of the other people could not (see Luke 2:29-38). Los Viejitos who dance before the Infant Christ enflesh the joy of Simeon's song, "My eyes have seen your salvation, a light of revelation to the pagans and the glory of Your people Israel" (Luke 2:31-32).

How can one keep doing the inner dance as the boy begins to stiffen? What types of social dances have been done by each different generation represented in the Church? How have these been part of their dance of life offered to the Christ? This story of Los Viejitos implies that in the end, we have no wealth but only the dance of life to bring before God.

The Beauty Way
The Navajo Yeibichai, Night Chant, or Beauty Way Ceremony as it may be called, is not connected with Christianity, but involves an attitude toward persons and the cosmos that could enrich Christian worship. Basically it is a ritual to pray that a sick person might be

cured, but underlying it is the interconnectedness of all people and creation. All gather because they are affected by and concerned about the sick person. This is another way of expressing St. Paul's idea that when one member of the Body of Christ suffers, all are affected in some way. In seeking healing and wholeness it is important to think about the people's relationships with many powers and aspects of creation. The ritual involves pollen, breath, feather wands, fire, incense, earth painting, evergreens, medicine plants, grass, cornmeal, rings of sumac, and it lasts eight and a half days. The ritual expresses the whole cosmological understanding of the Navajos: the value of tiny pollen, of flowers, of rain, of corn, and the importance of the community joining together to think good thoughts and to focus prayerful energy. Again and again chants similar to the following are repeated:

> Today I shall recover.
> Happily may I walk.
> May it be happy before me.
> May it be happy behind me.
> May it be happy below me.
> May it be happy above me.
> With happy all around me, may I walk.
>
> Restore my feet for me.
> Restore my legs for me.
> Restore my body for me.
> Restore my voice for me.
> My body feeling cold, may I walk.
> No longer sore, may I walk.
> With lively feelings, may I walk.
>
> The corn comes up, the rain descends.
> Vegetation comes.
> the rain descends, the corn comes up.
> The pollen comes.
> He arrives for you.
> He comes to the door.
> He enters for you.
> "Your body is strong,
> Your body is now holy," he says.
>
> Happily may fair goods of all kinds,
> To the ends of the earth come with you.
> With these all around you,

Happily may they come to you.
In beauty I walk.
With beauty before me I walk.
With beauty behind me I walk.
With beauty below me I walk.
With beauty above me I walk.
With beauty all around me I walk.
It is finished in beauty.
It is finished in beauty.
It is finished in beauty.

The ritual involves surrounding the sick person with beautiful scents, colors, songs, plants, dances, and caring people. Can beauty cure someone? Most of us would say no, yet when a person is in the hospital, often instead of sending something "useful" like food, money, medicine, or clothes, we send them flowers. Beauty is nourishment and medicine for the whole person.

The poetry of the Navajo ceremony might be a source of inspiration for a Christian healing service. The words could be mimed with a soft drum beat in the background. The congregation could be invited to open their hands to receive the beauty of God and then to bring it into their hearts. Another way to use the text would be as a dismissal chant in a regular service. The congregation would be invited to move out slowly, trying to have a sense of walking "in beauty" with that beauty spilling out of the doors of the church into their daily lives.

Good Christian ritual should be sensitive to the power of the lovely to bind up the wounds of those who come to services after a week of dealing with the practical which is often stripped of beauty. Ritual should allow persons to center themselves, to regain eyes and ears to see, beauty they may have missed. Ritual should lead persons to celebrate this beauty not just in their souls but in their whole bodies — that is, it should lead them to dance.

In Christian worship the people are the primary symbol; however, worship has often focused more attention on things than on the community. Today we are reminded: "Among the symbols with which liturgy deals, none is more important than this assembly of believers," and "the Sunday eucharistic assembly is the most fundamental ecclesial symbol."[6] What if on a certain day we decided not to use things but only people for worship, neither building nor organ, nor books, cross, candles, neither bread nor wine. What if we were to say to the congregation: "Each of you look at your own body. All of you look at each other. You are one body in Christ and individually members one of another' (Romans 12:4). You are 'living stones making a spiritual house' (I Peter 2:5). You are 'God's work of art created in Christ Jesus' (Ephesians 2:10). The word of God is written in your hearts (see Jeremiah 31:33). 'You are the light of the world' (Matthew 5:14). Your daily life is the bread which is to be broken for those who are hungry, needy, and weak."

Could we recognize God as we looked at our own bodies and our daily lives, or would we quickly want to get back the material objects, the building, the bread, the wine, the books, the art, and the candles, because we could not bear the responsibility of incarnate Christianity? To keep the things used in worship from becoming idols we must focus more and more on the action of the assembly. The Bishops' Committee on the Liturgy notes: "The most powerful experience of the sacred is found in the celebrating and the persons celebrating, that is, it is found in the action of the assembly: the living word, the living gestures, the living sacrifice, the living meals. This was at the heart of the earliest liturgies."[7] Using movement, gestures, and dance with an assembly of believers is a way of having them focus on God present in them, and not on the material objects of worship which can become idols. While Jesus is present in the bread in church we can focus on that as a distraction to keep us from recognizing His real presence in our bodies which go out into the market places, streets, factories, homes, parks, offices, schools, theaters, and hospitals. Today Jesus uses our hands to serve bread, to wash feet, and to touch lepers, and he uses our feet to take good news, to seek sinners and to dance canticles.

One of the principal aims of this text is to encourage the reader to explore human experiences and activities as the locus of meeting God. Las Canacuas deals with hospitality, Los Viejitos with aging, El Venador with sacrifice for another, processions with movement and journeys, Dance of the Four Directions with orientation, the Beauty Way with vision, sensitivity, and healing, the Matachines with centering through repetition, and La Tortuga with the life cycle. When we focus on, explore, and ritualize human activities and experiences such as hospitality, aging, sacrifice, traveling, and healing, we integrate daily life with prayer. These dances are not meant as extraneous things to be stuck in Christianity; rather, these dances, whether in education or worship, are meant to be magnifying glasses to help us perceive more clearly that all human experience can reveal the divine.

This book not only gives examples of Mexican and Native American dances, but suggests a way of looking at themes and forms of folk dances and learning to recognize in them "seeds of the Word," to use the expression of St. Justin Martyr. Dances and arts of all cultures can be explored in this way. Paul Ricoeur has urged that Christians claim a "postcritical naivete." Jesus instructed us to seek the truth, so it is appropriate to study literary criticism of scripture and academically articulated insights of contemporary theology. Jesus also urges us to "be as little children" and to be guileless as doves, to delight in simple things. We need both developed theologies and simple devotion. While the highly developed academic traditions of modern and ballet dance can contribute significantly to our liturgies, so can the folk traditions. In their spontaneity and naiveté they can help us to look, laugh, move, and clap our hands, to be as little children.

In the Christian community when people are invited to respect material creation rather than dominate it, or to use their bodies in worship instead of deny them, they often cry out in anger. The very intensity of these cries indicates how much healing is needed in these areas. A doctor can touch healthy parts of a patient's body and get no response, but when touching the sore area of a wound or broken bone, the patient cries out. When cries of protest are heard in Christianity, we can turn away from our brothers and sisters and allow the woundedness and brokenness of alienation from the physical to continue. On the other hand, we can, as Jesus in relating to the woman with the hemorrhage, invite people to acknowledge that we have been embarrassed about our bodies in the past (see Luke 8:43-48). We have thought that our bodies were unclean while our souls were good. Jesus not only affirmed and restored the woman's body but he wanted her explicitly and publicly to praise God in her renewed body. Using our whole body in public prayer is a way of both claiming and sealing the healing Jesus brings to us.

As we bind up the wounds separating our souls from our bodies, we must also bind up the wounds separating persons from other living things and the earth. Many of us live in contemporary environments in which we can have light in the dark, warmth in winter, coolness in summer, and dryness in the rain. In a way we have subdued the discomforts of nature, but in these realms where the realities of nature have been negated, we can lose our abilities to feel. We can become insensitive and numb. Dance that springs from peoples close to the earth can help mark a pathway back to the earth for those who live in synthetic environments estranged from creation. The dances of the waters, of the forests, of the fish, and of the animals are sacred and praise the Creator. Let us begin to contemplate, begin to see and hear them. Let us learn their dances and dance with creation.

Notes

[1]Bishops' Committee on the Liturgy, *Art and Environment for Catholic Worship* (Washington, DC: United States Catholic Conference, 1978), p. 22.

[2]Ibid., p. 15.
[3]Ibid., pp. 14-15.
[4]Ibid., p. 14.

[5]Ibid., p. 15.
[6]Ibid., pp. 18, 34.
[7]Ibid., p. 18.

About the Author

Martha Ann Kirk, CCVI, an Incarnate Word Sister of San Antonio, Texas, has been associate professor of Religious Studies and of Art as well as Campus Minister at Incarnate Word College. She holds an M.A. in Art Education from the University of New Mexico in Albuquerque and an M.A. in Religion and Religious Education from Fordham University in New York. She integrates dance, art, and drama in her ministry work and has been regional director of the Sacred Dance Guild. She was invited to give a workshop on liturgical dance in Mexico City, one of the first to be held in that country. Currently she is completing a doctorate in Theology and the Arts at the Graduate Theological Union in Berkeley.

Resources

Ballet Folklorico de Bellas Artes: Discos Musart (Musican Records Co., P.O. Box 75, Hialiah, FL). This record has short selections from thirty songs danced by the Ballet Folklorico de Mexico with full orchestration.

Children's Songs of Mexico: World Culture Series, ed. by Roberta McLaughlin and Lucille Wood (Bowmar/Noble Publishers, Inc., 4563 Colorado Blvd., Los Angeles, CA 90039, 1964). This record has explanations for children and short adapted selections including two songs associated with Posadas and "Bura Bampa," a part of the Yaqui Deer dance.

Christianity and Culture : by Virgil Elizondo (Huntington, IN: Our Sunday Visitor, 1975). This is a general introduction to pastoral theology and ministry in the Mexican American community. Elizondo notes the importance of the arts in culture and worship.

Dancing Christmas Carols: edited by Doug Adams (San Jose: Resource Publications, 1978). This book gives suggestions of how people of all ages can move as they sing Christmas carols and truly enflesh the Word. The book also describes choreography for carols for soloists and dance choirs.

Faith Expressions of Hispanics in the Southwest: Volume I (San Antonio: Mexican American Cultural Center, 1979). This report of a workshop facilitated by Spanish liturgist, Luis Maldonado, is a good guide for understanding popular piety and how it can be used in relation to the liturgy.

Folk songs of Latin America: World Culture Series #145; ed. by Roberta McLaughlin, B-102 LP (Bowmar Records, Inc., 622 Rodier Drive. Glendale, CA 91201, 1965). This record has explanations for children and short adapted selections of songs including an Aztec hymn to the sun, and two songs associated with Posadas, "Humildes Peregrinos" and "La Pinata."

Misa Criolla: by Ariel Ramiréz; Philips recording, Stereo PCC619. This record includes *Navidad Nuestra,* a folk drama of the nativity, which could be used for Los Pastores dances. It also has parts of the Mass sung in Argentinian folk music styles which are good for dance.

Modern Mayan: The Indian Music of Chiapas, Mexico: recorded by Richard Anderson; Folkways Record Album # FE 4377 (Folkways Records and Service Corp., 43 West 61st St., New York, 1975). This record of haunting authentic music from remote villages may appeal more to the professional anthropologist or musician than to the ordinary American, but it expresses the deep spirituality of the natives. It includes chanted prayers and music from religious fiestas.

Musica Prehispanica y Mestiza de Mexico: Estereofonico MKS-1773, RCA Victor Mexicana. This is an excellent record of improvisions on authentic prehispanic instruments as used by indigenous peoples. It includes a number of Conchero dances and ocarina, flute, chirimias, and percussion music suitable for many dances suggested in this book.

A New Direction for Catechetics and Liturgy for the Mexican American: by Angela Erevia, M.C.D.P. (San Antonio: Mexican American Cultural Center, 1978). This describes popular lore and piety of the Mexican American community and how these can be integrated with a liturgical and scriptural spirituality today.

Posadas: by Sister Celestine Castro (San Antonio: Mexican American Cultural Center). Booklet and cassette tape with "Posadas" and other Christmas songs in Spanish. This collection includes the traditional songs of Mary and Joseph asking for lodging, and contemporary prayers.

Rosas del Tepeyac: a Mass in honor of Our lady of Guadalupe, composed by Carlos Rosas (San Antonio: Mexican American Cultural Center). Record, songbook in Spanish. The songs include both the prehispanic and colonial styles of music. A photograph on the cover shows how the music has been danced in the Mass.

Regional Dances of Mexico: by Edith Johnston (National Textbook Co., 8259 Niles Center Rd., Skokie, IL 60076, 1974). Book in Spanish and English with a cassette tape of music. This book of skits for

Spanish classes contains detailed directions and music for a number of dances including Los Viejitos and Las Canacuas.

Ritual of the Wind: North American Indian Ceremonies, Music, and Dances: by Jamake Highwater (New York: Viking Press, 1977). This book by a Native American describes in detail six rituals including the Beauty Way and the Yaqui Easter Festival. It has many photographs and gives insight into native spiritualities.

Sing and Rejoice!: compiled and edited by Orlando Schmidt (Scottdale, PA: Herald Press, 1979). This book of congregational hymns from this century tries to express the universality of Christianity. The book has not only Native and Latin American music and negro spirituals from this continent, but also selections from China, India, Zaire, Tanzania, Sri Lanka, Israel, Jamaica, Indonesia, Fiji Islands, South Africa, West Indies, and other places.

Tapestry: a half-hour documentary movie of Rosa Guerrero, a Mexican American teacher in El Paso, who uses dances to understand and appreciate peoples of different cultures. It is available from Junior Women's Club, Tapestry, 1400 N. Mesa, El Paso, TX 79902, and from many school and denominational audio visual libraries in the southwest.

A Treasury of Mexican Folkways: by Francis Toor (New York: Crown Publishers, 1979). This popular book gives hundreds of pages of information on the history, arts, and customs of Mexico, including text and music of many songs and pictures of some dances.

Bibliography

Adams, Doug. *Congregational Dancing in Christian Worship.* Austin: The Sharing Company, 1971.

Amalorpavadass, D.S. *Gospel and Culture.* Bangalore: National Biblical, Catechetical, Liturgical Centre, 1976.

Artes de México. Ballet Folklórico de México. Numero 88&89, Ano XIV, 1967, 2a, Epoca.

Backman, Eugene Louis. *Religious Dances in the Christian Church and in Popular Medicine.* London: Allen and Unwin, 1952.

Bahti, Tom. *Southwestern Indian Ceremonials.* Flagstaff: K.C. Publications, 1970.

Bishops' Committee on the Liturgy. *Environment and Art in Catholic Worship.* Washington, DC: National Conference of Catholic Bishops, 1978.

Brodrick, James, S.J. *Saint Ignatius Loyola.* New York: Farrar, Straus, and Cudahy, 1956.

Covarrubias, Luis. *Regional Dances of Mexico.* Mexico, D.F.: Eugenio, 1979.

Fergusson, Erna. *Dancing Gods, Indian Ceremonials of New Mexico and Arizona.* Albuquerque: University of New Mexico Press, 1931.

Fisher, Constance. *Dancing the Old Testament.* Edited by Doug Adams. Austin; Sharing Company, 1980.

Gillmore, Frances. *Spanish Texts of Three Dance Dramas from Mexican Villages.* Tucson: University of Arizona Bulletin, Vol. XIII, No. 4, October 1, 1942.

Guidelines for a Texas Mission: Instructions for the Missionary of Mission Concepción in San Antonio (ca. 1760). Transcript of the Spanish Original and English Translation with Notes by Fr. Benedict Leutenegger, O.F.M. San Antonio: Old Spanish Missions Historical Research Library at San José Mission, Inc., 1976.

Hernandez, Joanne Farb, and Hernandez, Samuel R. *The Day of the Dead*. Triton Museum of Art, 1979.

Highwater, Jamake. *Dance, Rituals of Experience*. New York: A & W Publishers, Inc., 1978.

Ivanova, Anna. *The Dancing Spaniards*. London: Baker, 1970.

Kirstein, Lincoln. *The Book of the Dance*. Garden City: Garden City Publishing Company, 1942.

Laubin, Reginald and Gladys. *Indian Dances of North America*. Norman: University of Oklahoma Press, 1977.

Madsen, William. *Christo-Paganism, A Study of Mexican Religious Syncretism*. Doctoral dissertation. Berkeley: University of California, 1955.

Management of the Missions in Texas. *Fr. José Rafael Oliva's Views Concerning the Problem of the Temporalities in 1788*. Transcript of the Spanish Original and English Translation by Fr. Benedict Leutenegger, O.F.M. Introduction and Notes by Fr. Marion A. Habig, O.F.M. San Antonio: Old Spanish Missions Historical Research Library at San José Mission, Inc., 1977.

Menestrier, Claude Francois. *Des Ballets Anciennes et Modernes selon les regles due theatre*. Paris: Guignard, 1682.

Momprade, Electra y Tonatiúh Gutiérrez. *Historia general del arte mexicano, danzas y bailes populares*. Mexico: Editorial Hermes, S.A., 1976.

Museum of New Mexico. *Handbook of Indian Dances*. Santa Fe: Museum of New Mexico, 1952.

Pill, Albert Seymour. *Mexican Regional Dances for the Elementary School*. M.A. Thesis in Education. Los Angeles: University of California, 1963.

Poveda, Pablo. "Evtrevista con Andrés Segura." *Revista Rio Bravo*. Limited edition, Vol. 2, No. 2 (1981).

Ray, Sr. Mary Dominic, O.P., and Engbeck, Joseph H., Jr. *Gloria Dei, The Story of California Mission Music*. Berkeley: University Extension, 1975.

Robb, John Donald. *Hispanic Folk Music of New Mexico and the Southwest*. Norman: University of Oklahoma Press, 1980.

Rock, Judith. *Jesuit Theater and Ballet in the Seventeenth Century*. Unpublished paper.

Sachs, Curt. *World History of the Dance*. Translated by Bessie Schonberg. New York: W.W. Norton & company, 1937.

Sorell, Walter. *Music in the Southwest, 1825-1950*. San Marino, CA: Dunlap, 1967.

Swan, Howard. *Music in the Southwest, 1825-1950*. San Marino, CA: Huntington Library, 1952.

Taylor, Margaret Fisk. *A Time to Dance*. Philadelphia: United Church Press, 1967.

Other Resources for Worship from:

Dance

Actions, Gestures, and Bodily Attitudes
by Carolyn Dietering **$9.95**
Dancing Christmas Carols *edited by Doug Adams* **$7.95**
A Dancing People *by Adelaide Ortegel, SP* **$8.95**

Stories and Dramas

Winter Dreams and Other Such Friendly Dragons
by Joseph Juknialis **$6.95**
When God Began In The Middle *by Joseph Juknialis* **$6.95**
In Season And Out *by Bruce Clanton, SDS* **$6.95**
The Stick Stories *by Margie Brown* **$6.95**
Parables For Little People *by Larry Castagnola, SJ* **$6.95**
A People Set Apart *by Jean Gietzen* **$5.95**
How The Word Became Flesh *by Michael Moynahan, SJ* **$9.95**

Prayers In Poetic Form

Psalms of The Still Country *by Ed Ingebretsen, SJ* **$6.95**
God of Untold Tales *by Michael E. Moynahan, SJ* **$4.50**
God of Seasons *by Michael E. Moynahan, SJ* **$4.50**
Now Will I Sing *by Gerald Colvin, PHD* **$6.95**

Continuing Education

Modern Liturgy covers every aspect of the liturgical arts in worship. Nine issues per year, $27.

Family Festivals covers ritual, prayer, customs, and traditions of interest to parents who are trying to adopt Christianity as a lifestyle. Six issues per year, $16.